Getting Value from Strategic Planning

Highlights of a Conference

Edited by Frank Caropreso

Conference Program Director
Walter B. Schaffir

A Report from The Conference Board

Contents

PART III: WHO OWNS THE PLAN— THE CORPORATION VS. THE SBU

PART IV: MAKING IT WORK IN THE MARKETPLACE

PART V: STRATEGY AND INTERNATIONAL CONSIDERATIONS

From the President

Successful strategic planning remains a vital role of top management in most businesses. Although there is no standard model of successful organization and process for this function, a firm's CEO and business unit leaders have increasingly become the designers and judges of their plans. Planning staffs have shrunk or been dispensed with, but are vitally necessary to help general management as it plans, executes and evaluates.

Many more operating managers have become involved in the process. But not withstanding the participation of more people, we see an increase of comprehensive and flexible planning as well as a shorter time span between concept and execution. No one finds it easy to construct a design for the future of a business that is both visionary and practical, but many are shooting at these goals.

Proof that strategic planning is alive and well in the real world of business is shown by the enthusiasm of the audience attending The Conference Board's 1988 Strategic Planning Conference. This report represents the highlights of presentations from that meeting. The conference was planned and the speakers selected by Walter B. Schaffir. The Board appreciates the willingness and openness of the speakers who shared their experiences, insights and ideas with other executives.

JAMES T. MILLS
President

Who's Who Among Contributors

ROBERT J. ALLIO, President, Robert J. Allio & Associates

Dr. Allio provides management counsel to organizations in both the private and public sectors. He has led top level corporate strategy and management education projects for numerous organizations in the U.S. and abroad. Until 1979 he was affiliated with Arthur D. Little. Previously, as President of Canstar, he managed a portfolio of ventures in fiber optics, medical instrumentation, semiconductors, and consumer electronics. From 1968 to 1975 he was Director of Corporate Planning and Development at Babcock and Wilcox. Currently, he is advisory editor of *Planning Review*. His most recent book, *The Practical Stategist*, will be published in 1988. From 1981 until 1983 Dr. Allio was Dean of the School of Management at Rensselaer Polytechnic Institute. He is currently Professor of Management at Babson College.

KNUT R. BRUNDTLAND, Vice President, General Manager, Consumer Products Division, Robin Hood Multifoods Inc., Canada

Mr. Brundtland has profit responsibility for the Consumer Products Division of this Canadian company. Previously, he was Vice President for sales and marketing at H.B. Nickerson, Ltd. Before that, Mr. Brundtland served as Vice President and General Manager of Nabisco Brands Consumer Products (Canada).

VINCENT A. CALARCO, Chairman, President and Chief Executive Officer, Crompton & Knowles Corporation

Prior to 1985, Mr. Calarco was President of Uniroyal Chemical Company and Vice President of Uniroyal, Inc., having held previous positions of General Manager, Domestic Operations, and General Manager, Chemical and Polymers of the Uniroyal Chemical Company. Formerly, he was Business Manager, Plastics and Specialty Chemicals of NL Industries. Mr. Calarco is a Director of the Chemical Manufacturers Association, a member of Society of Chemical Industry and Societe de Chimie Industrielle, Chairman-Consultor Committee, Chemical Engineering, Manhattan College and a Trustee of Polytechnic Institute of N.Y.

RONALD B. CLARK, Senior Partner, Mallory and Associates

Mr. Clark joined Mallory and Associates in January, 1988. From 1985 to 1988 he was President and Chief Executive Officer of Jafra Cosmetics. From 1959 to 1985 he held various positions, including Vice President and corporate officer, at Avon Products, Inc.

JOSEPH L. DIONNE, President and Chief Executive Officer, McGraw-Hill, Inc.

Chief Executive Officer since April, 1983 and President since August, 1981, Mr. Dionne joined McGraw-Hill Book Company in 1967 as Vice President for Research and Development at the Educational Developmental Laboratories. Mr. Dionne was named Executive Vice President-Operations of McGraw-Hill in 1979, with executive responsibility for supervision, administration, and coordination of all revenue-producing operations. Prior to McGraw-Hill, his experience included teaching, educational administration, and consulting on a number of experimental education projects.

ELLEN M. HANCOCK, IBM General Manager, Communication Systems, International Business Machines Corporation

Having joined IBM as a programmer in 1966, Mrs. Hancock was elected an IBM Vice President in September, 1985. In December, 1985, she was named Vice President, Telecommunications Systems, Communication Products Division. She assumed the Presidency of the Communication Products Division in October, 1986, and her present position in January, 1988.

SUKEYUKI INABA, President, Asahi Chemical Industry America, Inc.

Prior to his present position, held since 1981, Mr. Inaba was General Manager, New Products Development, Fibers and Textiles, at Osaka Headquarters, Asahi Chemical Industry Co. (1979-1981). He is a Director of the Japanese Chamber of Commerce of New York, Inc.

WARREN J. KEEGAN, President, Warren J. Keegan Associates, Inc

Warren J. Keegan Associates specializes in assisting clients in global marketing and competitive strategy formulation and implementation, and in the design and delivery of executive educational development programs. Dr. Keegan is Professor of International Business and Marketing and Executive Director, Institute for Global Business Strategy, Pace University, and Adjunct Professor, Columbia Business School. Before founding his own firm, he was a consultant with Boston Consulting Group and Arthur D. Little, and marketing staff analyst, Pontiac Motor Division, General Motors Corporation.

WORTH LOOMIS, President, The Dexter Corporation

President of The Dexter Corporation since 1970, Mr. Loomis was previously Vice President of Finance and Director of Medusa Corporation. He is a Director of CIGMA Funds Group, Connecticut Natural Gas Corporation, and The Southern New England Telephone Company; a Director and Vice Chairman of Life Technologies, Inc.; a member of the Chemical Bank National Advisory Board; and Trustee and Chairman of The Strategic Planning Institute.

PAUL B. MARKOVITS, President-Avon Direct Selling-U.S. Division, Avon Products, Inc.

Mr. Markovits is responsible for all marketing, operations, sales, distribution, and research and development of Avon's Direct Selling-U.S. Division. With Avon since 1968, he was elected a vice president in 1981 for U.S. Operations and for International in 1984. He became Executive Vice President for all U.S. sales, distribution, marketing and operations in 1985.

L. DAVID MOORE, President and Managing Director, Interchem Inc.

Dr. Moore has held his present position since 1984. Previously, he was Executive Vice President of St. Regis Paper, Senior Vice President of Occidental Chemical Company, Vice President and Director of Chemetron Corporation, and Vice President, Petroleum Division of Nalco Chemical. Dr. Moore is a former Chairman of the New York State Council on Economic Education.

S. MORGAN MORTON, President, Warner-Lambert Canada

Mr. Morton was named to his present position in 1988. Prior positions at Warner-Lambert were President of the General Diagnostics Division, President and CEO of Warner-Lambert Puerto Rico, and Director of Corporate Strategic Planning. Mr. Morton was President and CEO of Organon Teknika Corporation from 1985 to 1986. He is a member of AMA's Presidents Association.

WALTER B. SCHAFFIR, President, Growth Dynamics, Inc.

Mr. Schaffir's career spans top-level posts with three major companies over two decades. As head of planning at Western Union, Continental Copper & Steel, and the Sperry Gyroscope Division of Sperry Rand, his reponsibilities included planning and development, administration, and staff support. Growth Dynamics, Inc., which Mr. Schaffir founded in 1971, is a consulting firm in business strategy and corporate planning. He organized and is Chairman of this Tenth Annual Conference on Strategic Planning.

D. KENT TIPPY, Group Vice President, Soabar Products Group, Avery International

Mr. Tippy has overall P&L and strategic direction responsibility for the Soabar Group of Companies. Previously, he was Corporate Vice President for Marketing and Strategic Planning and Vice President and General Manager of the Consumer Products Division. Earlier, Mr. Tippy held various marketing and management posts at General Mills (1968-1979).

GERARDO R. UNGSON, Professor, Graduate School of Management, University & of Oregon

Professor Ungson is also currently a visiting professor at Nijenrode, The Netherlands School of Business. He has taught at Dartmouth's Amos Tuck School, the University of California at Berkeley, and Pennsylvania State University. His forthcoming book, Competitive Strategies in High-Technology, is based on a three-year study of 18 firms in Silicon Valley.

JAMES R. WESSEL, President, Worldwide Glove SBU, Becton Dickinson and Co.

Mr. Wessel is responsible for coordinating and administering the industrial, medical, and consumer glove program of the corporation. Previously, he was President of Becton Dickinson's Edmont Division (1984-1987), President of Edmont Canada (1977-1984), and General Manager, Manufacturing at DMCO Industries Ltd.

Introduction

Walter B. Schaffir
President
Growth Dynamics, Inc.
Strategic Planning Conference Program Director

A few years ago, we were told by some best-selling authors that what makes for success in business is "A Passion for Excellence," and they had cases to prove it. Now we are told, by one of these same authors, that there are no consistently excellent companies. Times and circumstances have changed, and what is needed now is the ability to "Thrive on Chaos." Now, this makes me feel right at home. It certainly sounds like a whole lot more fun. After all, anybody knows what it takes to be excellent, but to thrive on chaos requires real management skill!

Seriously, however—managing under chaos is at the heart of the matter. The world of business is not neatly arranged; it never was. That's why so many of us had so much trouble with strategy development for so long. Strategy development is not a neat ten or 12-step process, as so many seminar brochures would have you believe. Plans are never executed just as they were conceived. It is our desire for simplistic solutions that leads us to unrealistic expectations.

And so strategic planning has gone through many stages. It's been formalized and systematized, criticized, reshaped, misunderstood, oversold (and overbought), once again redefined, misapplied, discarded . . . and revitalized. Today, strategic planning is alive and well in the real world of business. Still—strategic planning had gotten a bad name in some quarters—and often deservedly so. Frequently the cause was the perfunctory nature of the "exercise," which is just what it was: an exercise without real meaning. Frequently, it was the burdensome and time-consuming paperwork that served little real purpose. Often, it was the narrow view of what strategy means, as in the well-known *Fortune* articles that equated strategy merely with the famous Matrix and its celebrated shortcomings. And then there are those who insist that the concept of "strategy" applies only to the most grandiose of schemes. All of which is to say: Don't get trapped by words and fashions.

The papers in this volume focus on a simple term, value. What aspects of strategy development and implementation planning are helpful to managing a business? What aspects are largely meaningless effort? To get value from strategic planning, we must focus on sound strategic *thinking*—as opposed to merely generating planning-related paperwork. What is meant by "strategic thinking" and how does it differ from other ways of thinking about the business? And having decided what we mean by strategic thinking, how do we get the organization to do it? Certain key questions—hard to duck no matter what business you are in—are helpful in stimulating even the most cynical of managers to think strategically:

1. What is likely to upset your expectations? And what might be its impact if it happened?
2. What are your competitors up to? What are they doing differently? What does this mean to you?
3. What important opportunities are you currently foregoing?

Even the most tough-minded, bottom-line oriented executive wants answers to those questions. Yet, there is no way to address questions like these without becoming deeply involved in matters of strategy. The ensuing discussion is not about some esoteric notion of planning but about threats, opportunities, issues, and choices that face us on a daily basis.

The following presentations are intended to show how strategic planning contributes value to business operations in a variety of situations—and how it is affected by human values and organizational interplay.

Part I
Thinking Strategically

Thinking and Acting Strategically

Robert J. Allio
President
Robert J. Allio & Associates, Inc.

Many managers can no doubt recall—with pain and sorrow perhaps—instances when they or their organizations failed to develop a good strategy. Or had a good strategy that failed to work. Fewer managers can recall when they identified a clear and potent strategy and implemented it successfully. These rarer episodes are examples of strategic behavior. True strategic behavior has a number of salient characteristics that can be recognized and fostered within organizations. The success that managers have in promoting strategic behavior will determine how much they can improve business and corporate performance.

Stages of Strategic Behavior

My model for strategic behavior (see figure 1, p. 4) has four stages:

A. *Strategy Formulation*—identifying a potential sustainable competitive advantage. (A prerequisite to successful strategy formulation is the ability to think strategically.)

B. *Activation*—making a commitment to the strategy and allocating resources to effectively support it.

C. *Implementation*—carrying out the strategy.

D. *Adaptation*—modifying strategy and programs in response to changing conditions.

Managers must direct attention to each stage of this process.

What is Strategic Thinking?

More frequently than not, organizations adopt a planning process and develop strategies by rote, without actually thinking strategically. Managers can significantly improve the value of their planning by better understanding and facilitating strategic thought within their organizations.

The characteristics that distinguish strategic thinking from operational thinking include differences in both perspective and focus. Strategic thinking is concerned with positioning the organization for economic and managerial renewal,

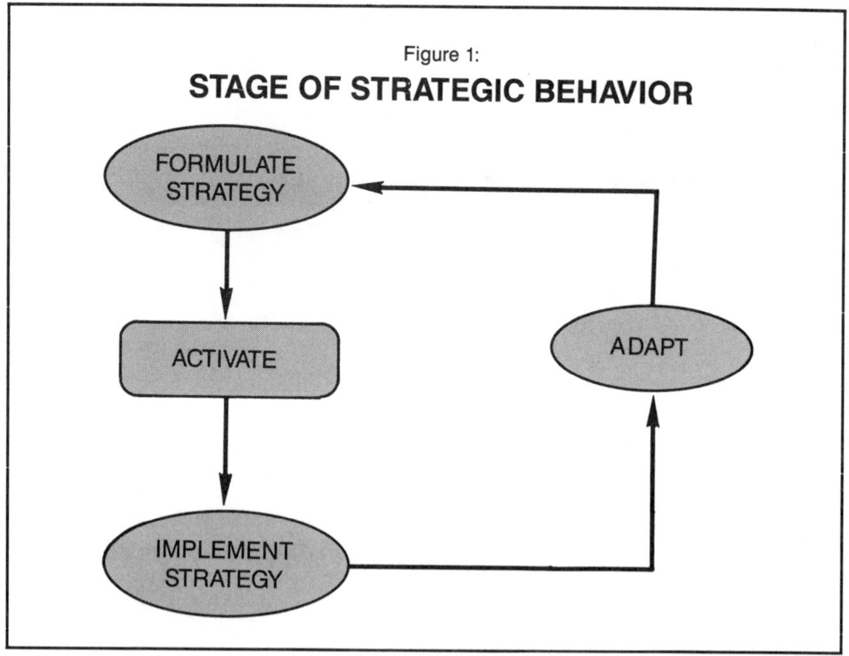

recognizing that the ultimate objective of strategy is to maximize shareholder value.

• Strategic thinking recognizes that survival depends more often upon responding to changes in industries and markets (forces outside the business), than upon maximizing internal effectiveness and efficiency. The quality of information systems related to the environment, for instance, must take precedence over internal productivity measurement systems (though these are also important).

• Strategic thinking recognizes the evolutionary nature of industries and markets. This is critical to learning from past experience, responding effectively to current challenges, and developing strategies that anticipate alternative future scenarios. The preoccupation of operational thinking with current conditions favors short-term responses and immediate results.

• Strategic thinkers focus upon the key success factors within their industries. Resources are targeted at these factors within particular markets that are expected to yield the desired results. Resource allocation in operationally minded organizations, on the other hand, is frequently dispersed; as a result, the firm serves no markets particularly well.

• Strategic thinking reflects the critical linkages among functional areas within the business and the importance of adding value in the entire chain, from raw-material sourcing through customer sales and service. Operational thinking tends to focus upon the effectiveness of each function, independent of other functions.

A ten-point program that managers can adopt to promote strategic thinking within their organizations follows:

1. *Study the competitors.* Some crucial questions include, "What are the competitors' strategies and relative performance?" and "How can I differentiate or change competitive equilibrium (even in small niches)?"

2. *Learn from customers and suppliers.* Managers should not rely simply upon their judgment about what satisfies customers or motivates suppliers. While intuition is valuable, it is no substitute for good information and strong relations. More often than not, stakeholders are willing to talk about their needs and strategies, particularly if doing so will result in improved products, service, or growth.

3. *Look for strategy peers.* Identifying firms that have complementary interests or strategies, especially in related markets or industries, can yield valuable opportunities to change the basis of competition or achieve competitive advantage. A powerful but often forgotten lesson is that industrial innovation, from copying to transportation, has invariably come from firms outside the existing industry.

4. *Identify and nurture distinctive competence.* The competence (relative to competitors) that a firm has in a functional area or in serving particular types of customers determines how successfully the firm can compete over the long term. Highly profitable businesses usually have leveraged a distinctive competence to give greater value to customers.

5. *Take a systemic view.* Recognizing the interdependence of functions within a business is critical to maximizing available resources and adding value. An appreciation of the linkages between an industry, its suppliers and customers is critical to anticipating or instigating changes. This can be particularly important in businesses where customer purchasing requirements and patterns are dictated by regulatory bodies, distribution channels, or other end-users.

6. *Accept change, discontinuity, and chaos.* Coping with change is a difficult task for any organization, but recognizing the inherent volatility of the world is the first important step in the process. Firms benefit greatly by establishing better environmental tracking systems to identify potential sources of discontinuity and vulnerability. Managers can then prepare contingency plans if the consequences of such vulnerability are likely to result in disaster.

7. *Study history.* The lessons of corporate history, even within a single organization, are rich with insight for those willing to learn. The advice of

history's great strategists (Sun Tzu, Musashi, Von Clausewitz) remains apropos in current times to all organizations.

8. *Challenge the current paradigm.* A good planning process incorporates mechanisms that offer managers the opportunity to challenge the conventional wisdom. Managers must ask themselves, "What alternatives do I have to break the rules, change the industry definition, or establish new alliances?"

9. *Develop alternative future scenarios.* Strategic thinkers have the ability to conceptualize alternative scenarios. Few managers would have predicted the impact that changes in markets and competitive conditions have had on U.S. industry during the past fifteen years (see figure 2). And the rate of change is accelerating. Today managers must ask themselves, "What will this industry look like in five years? What actions can we take to change that future?"

10. *Find a dominant theme.* No organization achieves distinction in the absence of a clear strategy, but a dominant theme or leitmotif can impel it to greatness and add meaning to its existence. A dominant theme serves still another role—an expression of corporate values and identity. When these values permeate the entire organization, strategy acquires meaning, and the members of the organization can commit themselves with enthusiasm and passion to it.

Activating Strategy

Many good strategies are never carried out. To close the circuit between strategy and implementation requires that the strategist be committed to action. Strategists often experience faint-heartedness or weak will—they conceive brilliant strategies, yet lack the energy, resolution, or courage to move forward.

Leaders can mobilize the energy of the organization behind a strategic vision or dominant theme. They bring an attitude that empowers the enterprise to move forward, to adapt, and to take risks. But even a strong signal from an enthusiastic leader will not suffice if the rest of the organization does not understand it and embrace it with fervor. An elegant strategic vision and clearly stated dominant theme will have no force unless the members of the organization align with the vision and share a commitment to implementation. CEOs can march off in any direction they please. But a brilliant visionary is likely to fail in an organization without the support of followers.

This raises the issue of appropriate goal setting for the organization. Goals that do not challenge the ability of the organization produce boredom. Excessively ambitious goals, on the other hand, produce anxiety, fear, or paralysis—they sap the morale and vitality of the organization. Aspirations must be set above the limits that may have been accepted previously.

Implementation

Those who have vision but no ability to realize their vision are dreamers—and their strategies can never be more than dreams unless they are implemented.

Figure 2:
CHANGING PARADIGMS

	OLD	NEW
Autos	large cars	compact cars
Electric Utilities	7% growth	2% growth
Textiles	low quality imports	high quality imports
Computers	mainframe	mini
Copying	centralized	decentralized
Consumer Electronics	service	reliability

(By the same token, those who have highly developed implementation skills but lack vision are merely mechanics.) Implementation requires managers and staff who are good at their trade, be it manufacturing, finance, marketing, or some other skill—who have mastered technique. Needless to say, these skills must be relevant to the task at hand, or they have no value. Translated into operational terms, the organization must be competent at carrying out programs that support its energy.

Performance will also suffer unless managers install congruent managerial systems—systems that support strategy implementation. Managerial systems including organization, information systems, measures of performance, and reward systems constitute the infrastructure of the firm. Implementation falters when the infrastructure gets in the way. It goes without saying that the characteristics of an organization's managerial systems influence strategy formulation as well as strategy implementation.

Adaptation

Contemporary organizations have embraced several myths. One of the most cherished is the myth of stability. Business as usual is a comforting notion, and organizations everywhere enjoy the feeling of safety that emerges when change is slow. Managers and planners, therefore, often direct themselves to the task of preserving the existing stable system and maintaining the status quo. Corporations everywhere exhibit a pernicious determination to persist in old strategies when the world has changed. The alternatives—modifying the system or allowing it to evolve—are not often contemplated.

Implicit in this world view is the myth of control. Many managers have the hubris to believe that they can control the environment—or at least those aspects of it that affect their business. The leaders of organizations devoted to stability commit maximum effort to improving forecasts in the belief that the firm can erect appropriate defenses and marshal enough resources to cope with whatever comes. But alas, planners repeatedly forecast the wrong discontinuities, and the future continues to resist definition; stability is a false idol. Like many other non-linear disorderly systems, businesses often experience major changes when the initial conditions change slightly.

Thus, even though a dominant theme can be timeless, the details of a strategy can rarely endure for more than a few years. Firms that cling to old missions (the railroads), to old values (autocratic management), or to obsolete paradigms (national competition) are particularly vulnerable to extinction. A superior organization requires the ability to sense change (or cause change) and adapt to it.

Stable systems are fail-safe—they minimize the probability of failure by introducing high negative feedback. But these policies often inhibit risk taking and entrepreneurship. Resilient systems by contrast are safe-fail—they minimize the consequences of failure. More important, the resilient system is consonant with evolution, ultimately the only certain strategy for survival. Thus railroads could become transportation companies, autocratic organizations could anticipate the need to become more participative, and parochial firms could enter global markets.

High-performing organizations transform themselves to meet future challenges. They achieve this adaptability by investing resources in activities that increase their future options. The most obvious vehicle for such investment is R&D, which multiplies the number of future product or process options and leads to economic renewal. Investments in management training and development are at least as important. These investments produce managerial renewal, particularly if they create the attitudes that foster innovation and thinking about the future—if they enable the organization to learn. And investments in strategic relationships are increasinly important. The firm with a network of alliances (with governments, suppliers, customers, competitors) can realize a competitive headstart when economic or political conditions change.

The Challenge of the 1990s

The next decade will challenge every manager in every organization to become more effective and more efficient—to think and act strategically, applying the principles of practical strategy. To summarize these principles:

• Enunciate a clear strategy and dominant theme. Make purpose and values clear.

• Activate the organization by making a conscious and deliberate personal commitment. Develop total organizational support for realizing the strategy.

• Install the right functional skills to assure that strategy can be implemented successfully. Establish managerial systems that support the implementation of strategy at every level. Satisfy the need for connections to all the stakeholders inside and outside the organization.

• Adapt quickly to the demands of dynamic environment, and respond quickly to opportunities and problems. Abandon yesterday's strategy or paradigm if a better one is revealed today. Look for the patterns that suggest new and more inspired responses to challenge.

True strategic behavior is rare—and strategic planning is commonly indicted as the culprit. Strategic thinking usually can be improved, but other elements of strategic behavior may actually be at fault. Superior performance, be it at the level of the corporation, the business, or the functional unit, arises from acting like a practical strategist: by thinking strategically, activating, implementing, and adapting.

Can the "Soft Side" of Strategy Development Be Managed?

Dr. Gerardo R. Ungson
Professor, Graduate School of Management
University of Oregon

When developing their business strategies, firms rarely use the rational and analytical procedures espoused in management textbooks. Moreover, it is widely acknowledged that even some of the best-conceived strategies fail to get implemented properly. Scholar and practitioners have suggested several reasons why such strategies fail:

- A lack of total commitment from top management;
- The absence of a structure to facilitate implementation;
- A reliance on disjointed or fragmented approaches to implementation;
- A failure to involve people directly involved in implementing strategy;
- Unrealistic implementation deadlines; and
- Opposition from powerful groups.

These reasons suggest that implementing strategy is a highly complex activity that involves the integration of human and organizational resources. I believe strategies also fail because planners often pay too much attention to the structure and the content of formal strategic plans and not enough to the informal organizational processes that underlie and generate them. Figure 1 depicts the differences in emphasis in what we may term the "hard" versus the "soft" side of strategy development. Unless strategic planners understand the organizational processes that generate strategies, it will be difficult for them to prescribe the right strategies.

Theory Versus Practice

Firms need to maintain a balance between formal strategic planning (theory) and informal implementation processes (practice). Formal strategic planning tends to be *purposeful*, *consistent*, and *rational*. Yet, strategic implementation tends to be *fragmented, evolutionary*, and *intuitive*. Although formal strategic planning is broadly adaptive and mostly routine, the implementation of strate-

Figure 1:

THE "HARD" VS. THE "SOFT" SIDES OF STRATEGY DEVELOPMENT

"HARD" EMPHASIZES:	*"SOFT" EMPHASIZES:*
• OVERALL GOALS OF THE CORPORATION	• POLITICS OF MULTIPLE COALITIONS
• CONTENTS OF STRATEGIC PLANS	• GENERATIVE PROCESSES OF COALITIONS
• INDUSTRY ANALYSIS	• EXTANT POLITICS
• STRATEGIC MAPPING	• TIME IMPERATIVES
• SUCCESS-REQUIREMENTS	• PREVIOUS HISTORY OF DECISIONS
• SCENARIO PLANNING	• PREFERRED "SOLUTIONS"
• STRUCTURE AND CONTENT	• POLITICS AND PROCESS

gies takes place in a confusing world—a world full of prosaic processes that can lead to surprising outcomes. Consequently, in practice, implementation deviates, from textbook prescriptions. Given this disparity, what is the value of formal planning? For the past three years, I have examined this issue by focusing on U.S. high-technology firms that are locked in competitives battles with their Japanese counterparts.

I found that the *real* strategies of these firms were rarely the result of formal strategic planning. Rather, formal strategic planning decisions provided a driving force that became interspersed with social and political forces to arrive at *actual* strategies. Even so, formal strategic planning provided:

- A formal basis for exchanging information;
- An opportunity for participants to examine underlying assumptions about competitors;
- Information on various types of risk;
- A forum in which participants could talk about "sensitive" issues in an indirect manner; and
- The baseline against which participants could test intuitions that would otherwise not be reflected in quantitative analyses.

Taken in this context, formal strategic planning plays an important role but not necessarily the one represented by traditional planning theories. Instead, formal planning provides participants with a sense of collective urgency, a means to challenge their respective assumptions, and an excuse to communicate—without delving into the actual content of the strategic plans.

Incremental Decisions

If actual strategies do not always result from formal planning, how do they come about? Decisions about strategies tend to be *incremental* and *evolutionary*, as opposed to *comprehensive* and *revolutionary*. As many have noted, the full consequences of key environmental events (e.g., oil shocks, Wall Street crashes, trade measures, etc.) are often difficult to predict and control. Accordingly, managers attempt to cope with the lead time demanded by major decisions by gathering information on these events, by overcoming informational and political barriers to change, and by creating personal and organizational awareness, acceptance, and commitment to the strategic response. Incremental decisions are not fraught with ambiguity and confusion, as once thought. If managed properly, they can be purposeful and lead to highly effective decisions.

Maintaining the proper balance between rational analysis and seasoned intuition can be done in several ways. First, companies must manage the incremental process in which strategies are enacted. Second, they must develop strong corporate cultures to accommodate the requirements of formal and informal planning. Third, based mostly on my own study of high technology firms, they must develop infrastructures that are flexible enough to meet the requirements of all corporate strategies.

Managing Incrementalism. Here are some specific steps in which to successfully manage the incremental process:[1]

1. Sensing needs. Effective managers try to sense the need for strategic change in nonspecific terms.

2. Building awareness without identifying specific actions or making specific commitments. This may involve the use of study groups and consultants.

3. Broadening support. Managers intensify the discussion of options and explore constructive movements without threatening the major centers of power.

4. Creating pockets of commitment. Options are tested in limited contexts, and conditions that create opportunities for the desired changes are explored.

5. Support is broadened and political opposition is tested.

[1]J. Brian Quinn, *Strategies for Change: Logical Incrementalism*, 1980.

6. Obtaining a real commitment. A project/idea champion emerges to carry out the desired changes, with supporters placed in positions of responsibility and opponents reassigned.

7. Building consensus. The desired change is formally announced and managers attempt to build consensus throughout the organization.

This incrementalist approach underscores the importance of coalitions in organizations. Coalitions arise because of differences in goals, perceptions, and priorities; they are enhanced by resource scarcity, limited information sharing, and task interdependence. The strategic process is not impervious to the political influences of various coalitions. Failures in strategic implementation may arise when changes are resisted by powerful coalitions within the organization. To be successful, firms need to manage the context as well as the process of strategic formulation.

Managing the Corporate Culture. It is widely accepted that corporate culture has a subtle but pervasive influence on individual behavior. To properly manage corporate culture, one has to be able to measure it well. Leading consultants have attempted to chart culture by collecting anecdotes, company stories and sagas, by inferring from written reports and memoranda; and by using formal questionnaires. The intent is to flush out the governing rules and norms, as opposed to those people profess or that are published in company manuals.

In dealing with corporate culture, the planner comes to grips with the soft side of strategy development. In a sense, corporate culture determines what planners *can* or *cannot* do. If a new strategy conflicts with deeply held, shared values in an organization, it is unlikely that it will succeed. On the other hand, a compatible strategy may be implemented with ease.

Developing Flexible Infrastructures. In studying high-technology firms, I found that they attempted to become resilient to their environments by developing infrastructures (i.e., cultures, processes, learning systems, governance, and basic support systems) that they believed would accommodate the requirements of *any* strategy.

There is a growing consensus that we might have overemphasized the content of formal strategic plans but not the organizational processes that generate them. These processes are as important, if not more so, than formal planning, and can be described in terms of incremental decisions that are logical and purposeful. The soft side of strategy development can be controlled through managing incrementalism, corporate culture, and building flexible infrastructures.

The Role of "Values" in Shaping Strategy

Worth Loomis
President
The Dexter Corporation

Organizations that successfully implement strategy share some common values or cultural components—they have internal agreement on what constitutes "success," they utilize support systems, and they appreciate and seize opportunities to profit.

Strategy implementation takes place in a confusing world. It's confusing for two reasons: first, because a number of the events that affect the organization we are trying to manage in a strategic way are random or beyond our control; and second, because the raw stream of information reaching us with reference to all events is massive, unordered, and yet inadequate.

One of the characteristics of a good manager is that he or she can stand in the middle of this confusing stream of information and select the data that is important, analyze it, and set an appropriate course of action. Training and experience improve the manager's ability to get the facts, analyze and decide, but the benefit to the corporation is greatly aided if all managers are in agreement on what constitutes success. Paul Ylvisaker of the Ford Foundation, for example, says that business people run highly complicated and efficient organizations that have a common and simple "value system"—profit.

Of course, getting everyone to act rationally on the notion that success equals profit isn't as simple as it sounds. We all know managers who judge success in terms of how many companies they acquire, how high they can build assets, how many machines are on the plant floor, or how many people report to them—none of which necessarily connects with profit.

The old-fashioned notion of profit is no longer an adequate description of success. Success today is defined as "the increase of shareholder value." This is not the same thing as the increase of sales, assets, shareholder's equity, book value, return on investment, or of earnings per share. There are some real differences between shareholder value and earnings per share. Shareholder value is concerned with:

- Cash flows and not accounting-measured flows;
- Maximizing cash flows over time and not maximizing the short term.
- The spread between the cost of capital and the return on capital, not the return itself. For example, a 15 percent return on a 10 percent cost of capital is much better than an 18 percent return on a 15 percent cost of capital. One

way to reduce your capital costs, as every raider knows, is to increase the ratio of debt to equity.

This is a sample of the kind of information you need to compile about each of your business units or segments. To get this kind of analysis on a regular basis, your finance departments will have to do some work they may not be enthusiastic about doing. But the corporate raider is out there, alive and lurking and running just such an analysis on the different units of your company and mine.

You and I need, therefore, to build an information system for managers that reports true measures of success. The corporate culture must reward the "value-biased" manager and not unwittingly invite the corporate raider to tender for the firm's stock.

Utilize Support Systems

What kind of support systems for strategy implementation does your firm have in place? Does your corporate culture reward risk taking? And does it tolerate some failure, since a system that punishes failure discourages risk taking? Have you a bonus system that rewards profitable growth that is biased toward value creation? Does it discourage unprofitable growth since unprofitable growth subtracts value from the enterprise and is one of the first things a raider looks for? Does your culture and bonus system support the implementation of strategy changes when they are necessary or are they geared to business as usual?

Before you can design systems that support your strategy, you must articulate your corporate mission, your long-range plans, goals, and strategies. Goals should be narrowly focused on areas in which the organization can have some sustainable competitive advantage.

Long-range planning is not a process that occurs for three days once a year at a New England resort. You need to have your long-range plan and your strategies in mind all the time, particularly before you prepare the next year's budget. Sometimes strategies have to be changed. After two or three years of no growth in the early 1980s, Dexter launched a New Directions program. We stopped business as usual in about a dozen product lines and plants with low returns and uncertain prospects, sold some off and liquidated others. We set about investing the proceeds in seven higher risk, higher growth, good businesses with sustainable competitive advantage, business areas we were already in and knew something about.

This kind of implementation of new strategies requires change and change requires champions. Champions must come first of all from the top of the corporation, but no less importantly they must be found and supported wherever corporate resources are allocated.

Seize the Opportunity

Pasteur said, "Chance favors the prepared mind." Since strategy implementation takes place in a confusing world, it is important to have prepared the mind of the corporation to recognize opportunity as it occurs. One of the purposes of well-done, long-range planning is to force reflection and preparation.

Most acquisitions, for example, are best made on an opportune basis. Be prepared to recognize opportunity when it appears in the marketplace. Acquisitions that are company specific rather than opportune generally result in a bidding war, which means an abnormally high price, and then require short-term payback in order to compensate for the purchase price. This may delight investment bankers and corporate raiders, but it rarely results in good grist for people who have to run operations.

But within the best of operations there are always choices, or unstable states, that provide opportunities for the alert manager: Choice between short and long term; between investment in internal development and the reporting of earnings per share; between the strategy that optimizes the business unit and the one that optimizes the corporation; and between pruning the organization and maintaining the team.

In general, if earnings are down, the work force is prepared for required changes—reorganizations that better align the operation with the requirements of strategy are accepted. If earnings are a little better than required, there will be an opportunity to fund some "skunk works"—projects that the front office never sees. When they work, everyone is happy; when they don't, no one knows about it. Whether it's an R&D project, a piece of software, or a consultant's report, skunk works are an opportunity to advance a strategy (although not always an officially approved one). By the way, shaving off earnings peaks with such projects has almost no downside; there is no penalty even if the projects fail. Stock price is determined by regular and expected (expected means low beta) cash flows, not by one-time earnings gains that increase cash and the stockholder equity on which you have to earn a return on investment.

Here are some examples of back-country wisdom that I have found useful:

• Tolerance of ambiguity is a useful managerial talent. Because of the confused nature of the world, you never know when today's truth will be tomorrow's mistake. Keep your options open. It is much better to be lucky than smart.

• Wrong action is better than no action. It is OK to tolerate ambiguity but don't be indecisive. Bela Gold of Case Western Reserve University has done productivity studies that show that wrong decisions by a unit, say a piece of new equipment that turns out to be a poor design, can bring forth a sustained surge of productivity that largely overcomes the error. Organizations need to perceive themselves as moving even if mid-course corrections are necessary later on.

• Put the facts in front of managers and employees or require them to get the answers to the right questions. They will draw the same conclusions from those facts as senior management, and they will act on their own conclusions much more responsibly than they act on dictates from the front office.

• And lastly, because the world is a confusing place, avoid the home-run mentality. Go for singles and doubles. Make a little, sell a little.

Part II
Formulating and Evaluating the Strategy

Creativity, Planning, and Running a Business

Joseph Dionne
Chairman and Chief Executive Officer
McGraw-Hill, Inc.

The need for strategic thinking in business is basic and clear, so I needn't sell you on the concept. The need for creativity in business is equally clear—and in today's extremely competitive environment, creativity has to exist throughout an organization. It has a vital role to play in managing, manufacturing, and marketing; in applying today's technologies to a company's operations; in giving an existing product new, added value for its customers; and in developing new products and services.

Sparking Creativity

Creativity provides that extra competitive edge that can bring that extra dollar to the bottom line. More important, it can have a real impact on the quality of the lives of our customers—and of our employees. So the question is: In the corporate environment, how can we combine the need for rigorous strategic thinking with the need for individual innovation? Clearly, there's no single answer. But I can tell you how we at McGraw-Hill have tried to combine them, and what we've learned from our efforts.

At first, we may seem an atypical corporation. Our heritage is publishing—which means writing, reporting, and editing. So, creativity has always been an important part of our work. But this type of work, too, can benefit from systematic strategic thinking. Like many companies, we have experimented in our strategic planning with various concepts—"cash cows and dogs," "product life cycles," "breadwinners," and others. But the process of planning is as important as the product, and the process must fit our corporate culture. So, some years ago, we introduced the concept of the "value-added chain" into our planning process. We have since determined that it best fits who we are and our mission to educate and inform.

The value-added chain defines six key steps that go into transforming raw data into quality information products. These are: collecting the data; storing it; processing it; transforming it (putting it into the form that will be most practical and convenient for its customers); disseminating it; and selling the resulting information. This concept applies to all of our products, regardless of their form, and has provided us with a powerful tool for analyzing the way our business runs. Moreover, it has helped us to develop new products. For example, by using the value-added chain concept, we learned how we could link two data bases, and blend and deliver them electronically. It has helped us to focus our resources on new opportunities, such as investing in a series of systems to help our staff develop, acquire, and market computer software. And, value-added has helped us manage and leverage our costs.

Planning for Change

Our application of strategic planning has been an important tool in helping us to grow as a corporation. And, as a corporation— expanding, adapting new information technologies and, in 1985, implementing a major reorganization as a corporation. We've had not only the challenge of maintaining our creativity but also of instilling a deeper, broader sense of entrepreneurship throughout the corporation.

Both McGraw-Hill and the information industry have undergone substantial changes in recent years. To understand these changes, it's useful to look back.

McGraw-Hill was founded in 1888 by James McGraw, and the company's first products were magazines. Later, he put articles from the magazines into book form, so books became the company's next product.

As the nation's needs for information changed, we sought to meet those needs with new services—and that's essentially how the company expanded. Starting in the 1960s, through acquisitions, we moved into four new fields: financial services with Standard and Poor's Corporation; construction information with the F.W. Dodge Corporation; broadcasting with the purchase of four television stations; and economic information through the acquisition of Data Resources, Inc. These businesses became the basis of our organizational structure. Each operated essentially as a separate company with its own specialized resources, serving its own specialized market niche. During the 1960s and 1970s this organizational structure served us well. But by the early 1980s, we saw four main trends beginning to reshape the information industry:

(1) Increasingly global markets for information. And an increasingly global impact for information, from financial data to oil prices.

(2) The need for information in many forms and frequencies. Some customers want a reference work updated annually; others might need value-added news delivered weekly (*Business Week* magazine); or up-to-the-minute information, delivered real time, on-line or through broadcast technology—or a combination of all these.

(3) An increasingly segmented marketplace for information—like the marketplace for so many of today's products and services. Business people want specific information—to serve a specific purpose or do a specific job—and in a form that permits them to put that information to immediate use.

(4) Rapid technological change. As computers and communications become increasingly available, their costs decrease and their capabilities increase. These

changes are bringing new competitors into the information marketplace, challenging our leadership.

To respond to these external forces, we had to make internal changes. We took a good look at our individual business units, their resources, and market niches and recognized that many were segments of broader industry groupings.

For example, we had several divisions in different parts of the corporation all serving the construction industry. In one of our operating companies, the F.W. Dodge division was providing project data and microfilmed building plans for builders and contractors. In the same operating company, another division was producing building-product information for architects. Another operating company was publishing five different magazines, from *Architectural Record* to *Engineering News Record*, now known as *ENR*. Still another, Data Resources, was providing demographic and statistical data and forecasts.

By bringing together such related business units we saw that we could create something that none could achieve alone: an immensely strong market position in their industries, powered by an extensive array of market-directed products and services. We envisioned McGraw-Hill as a huge, multimedia information resource, whose parts could be combined to meet the full information needs of our customers. And from a strategic point of view, we saw that move as a way to achieve more growth and higher revenues. So, in the beginning of 1985, we reorganized our operations into about 20 distinct market-focus groups.

It was the biggest change in the company's history. Once it was completed, with the market-focus concept in place, the stage was set to begin the next phase: expanding the reach of our market-focus groups; filling in the information gaps, through acquisitions; and introducing new products and enhancing existing ones. This is where we're drawing on our growing sense of innovation and working to developing creativity.

At McGraw-Hill, people are our most important resource. We realized that any change could only work if the people involved understood, supported, and, in short, took ownership of it.

One route was through a succession of meetings. Every two years, we bring together about 135 of our top management people for a three-day, off-site conference. Through speakers from inside and outside the corporation and breakout sessions, we tackle a broad range of subjects affecting our business. These may include deregulation; evolving information technology; our customers' changing information needs; and the strategies our various business units are planning to use to meet those needs.

In the summer of 1985, we devoted part of our conference to the subject of "intrapreneurship"—or adapting the spirit of entrepreneurship to the corporate environment. We had presentations on the subject by five of our people, who discussed intrapreneurship in terms of McGraw-Hill and how we, as managers, could adopt that concept to spark the development of new products and new markets.

Two months later, we held another meeting, for a broader management audience. It was one of a series of quarterly Management Forums, to which about

300 managers are invited. At that particular forum, we reported the highlights of the off-site conference, and we included the presentations by the McGraw-Hill managers on intrapreneurship.

Communication has played a tremendous part in spreading the message. For example, our employee newspaper reported the Management Forum, publicizing and promoting the concepts of intrapreneurship, creativity, and innovation to McGraw-Hill men and women all over the world.

During the months that followed, as we developed new products and services and introduced them to the marketplace, we also reported them in the company newspaper. We reported on our new publications, new PC software products, new on-line data feeds, our first video magazine, and our first computer conferencing service. We demonstrated how the "multimedia" concept was taking hold by describing how one of our book company units published its first magazine, how one of our magazines published its first book.

The communication process has been ongoing. Since the reorganization, we've introduced many new products and media, including real-time data services delivered by FM satellite and broadcast technology, and our brand new CD-ROM products. The idea is to reinforce creativity through straightforward reporting of how our employees are creating real products. The overall message is not that innovation exists but that innovation works.

We have yet another important message to convey. We want our people to know that innovation also pays. At McGraw-Hill, we give awards and cash rewards to employees who launch successful new products; enhance existing ones; use technology to create successful new product platforms, and demonstrate editorial excellence. These awards are presented at one of our quarterly Management Forums and are reported through the employee newspaper. Now, several of our operating companies, and divisions within the operating companies, have started similar recognition programs.

Creativity and strategic thinking are also fostered through our Corporate Human Resources Development programs. There are workshops on market strategy and growth strategy and programs on how to apply those strategies to product development, business planning, and assessing potential acquisitions. There are workshops on entrepreneurial and innovative management. We're also collaborating with the Graduate School of Business at New York University to develop case studies of our most successful launches, so we can disseminate that knowledge throughout our market focus groups.

When we began planning the reorganization, we saw the corporation as one huge multimedia provider of information. Thus, educating our people to think "multimedia" is another continuing step in promoting innovation. Since our customers want their information in a variety of forms, one challenge was to educate our staff about these forms, making our people comfortable with the broad range of media available to them. The goal is to help them in meeting customers' information needs, to think not in terms of just one way, but in terms of the best way.

Our "channel champion" program addresses this challenge. Each information delivery channel has been put under the wing of a McGraw-Hill manager who is responsible for encouraging the use of that medium in the planning and development of new products. Each channel champion is responsible for publicizing the availability and advantages of his/her medium to the rest of McGraw-Hill. Each has to be familiar with the technology, its producer, and who outside of McGraw-Hill uses it. The channel champion is responsible for scanning all of McGraw-Hill's business units and markets to see where that medium might be applied and then serving as an advisor to any business unit that wishes to use it.

It's an exciting program, and it's working wonderfully. The channel champions have conducted informative seminars, put on demonstrations, brought in outside speakers, put out newsletters—all in addition to their other, full-time responsibilities—but with added compensation.

Our Corporate Human Resources Development programs also deal with media. An important point is that these meetings on media—the ones by the channel champions and ones by Corporate Human Resources—are publicized ahead of time, and our entire staff is welcome to attend.

Some of the newest results of our creativity go on display each year at our Annual Meeting. Each market focus group has a booth to demonstrate its newest products, and each booth is staffed by people from the group. Other employees are welcome to come. It's fun to watch many managers use their coffee break to tour other booths. Often their eyes light up as they get a glimmer of new-product ideas for their own markets—and ideas for synergistic ventures with other units of the corporation as well.

Since we launched the market focus organization three years ago, we've developed a still-growing array of products and services. Over the past year alone, the number of projects in development, or beyond that in the test phase, has doubled. Clearly, not every product on the drawing board gets to market. We expect some failures—but that's part of the process. If we don't have failures, we're not properly encouraging our managers to be creative and to tackle new challenges.

How does fostering the creative spirit fit into the strategic planning process? At our company, the planning process moves from bottom to top. It starts with a business unit—with the managers who are on the firing line, who know their markets, and who have the profit-and-loss responsibility for meeting those markets' information needs. We then ask each of these units to look at its market niche in terms of:

- The size of the market and its growth potential;
- Who the customers are;
- What information customers need and how they use it;
- What we think their future information needs will be;

• Who else is serving that market and how we measure up against the competition.

We ask our business units to assess the opportunities—and the roadblocks—that will shape their success in their markets and to come up with their own strategic plans to accomplish their goals and succeed in their market niches. The plans for each separate business unit are then combined at the market-focus level, grouped for administrative purposes, and, finally, integrated into plans for each operating company.

For most corporations, strategic plans are annual plans, so a corporation is usually locked into it from January through December. What happens, then, if someone gets a creative idea in July? At McGraw-Hill, each of our operating companies budgets money for what we call a Venture Fund. The money is there if a business unit needs it—and can make a case for that need—to take advantage of a sudden opportunity to create a new product or a new business.

This was an important cultural change for us. Once, we were accused of being a rigid, control-oriented corporation, where everything costing more than $250,000 had to go upstairs for approval. That did not foster creativity. So, first we pushed the approval process down into the operating companies, then down even further to the market-focus level, where the products are devised. The market-focus managers know that opportunity is in their own hands; so is the risk, and to me that only sharpens their sensitivity to good planning.

The corporate planning function creates the structure within which the choices are made. One part of that structure is the definition of our corporate mission: We're multimedia providers of information. We're not, say, a cable company that might carry the information or a computer company that might distribute it from a mainframe to employees' personal computers. Over the years, we've made the strategic decision as to who we are. And that saves a lot of wheel spinning.

Another part of the structure consists of scanning the business environment for opportunities and roadblocks. At the corporate level, we develop a series of issues that we think each of our operating companies will face. We ask: What technologies will impact their markets and their customers? What's the economic outlook? What will be the political and social environment for the industries we serve? What is the regulatory outlook? And most important, what is the significance of these factors?

For example, assume a scan tells us there'll be a slowdown in the construction industry in two years. Does that mean builders will cut back on their spending for information—and that this part of McGraw-Hill's business will drop? Or could it mean an opportunity for us: Will builders need more or different kinds of information to help them find projects they can bid on? We look for an awareness in each of the operating companies' plans for recognition of such issues and for specific strategies to deal with them.

Scanning also ties in with our training programs. Our Corporate Human Resources Development department conducts sessions on strategic thinking, entrepreneurship, media and other subjects, as part of our effort to promote creativity. These are planned to tie in directly to what we at the corporate level see as our coming training needs.

Another important part of the planning structure that corporate management provides consists of financial goals and measurements. We set corporate targets over the near and long term for revenue growth, cash generation, level of investments, return on investment, and others. These goals, in turn, are translated into objectives for each of the operating companies.

You can set goals for revenue growth, and that's a fair measure for any operation. But in setting efficiency measures, the corporate planners have to understand the nature of each business in our portfolio. In the book business, a fair efficiency measure is return on assets—because you've got assets in the form of inventory, book plates, and so forth. In the magazine business, which depends on advertising, it's more appropriate to measure return on sales. So, it's important to differentiate. Differentiation is also important when it comes to allocating capital for reinvestment in the business and in acquisitions.

Overall, the strategic planning process becomes a joint effort—a creative exercise—where ideas, opportunities, and resources are reviewed, weighed, and balanced in favor of what's best for the corporation as a whole. For us, this process works well. But that doesn't mean it can't work even better.

McGraw-Hill is still evolving and our planning system has to keep pace. We're continuing to study how we can make strategic planning more flexible and responsive to changing environments—to make it a dynamic process that promotes not only growth for the corporation but also promotes growth, innovation and creativity within on the part of the people who create the plans that drive the company forward.

Getting Value from Plan Reviews

Knut R. Brundtland
Vice President and General Manager
Consumer Products Division,
Robin Hood Multifoods Inc., Canada

I believe that the most important element in a successful plan review is the plan itself. If the plan is inarticulate, lacks specific actions to be taken, and is based more on assumptions than facts, the review will be foggy. It will turn into a debate rather than an evaluation and become a rehash of the plan rather than a critical examination of what has actually taken place in relation to what was envisioned.

I suspect that the advice "Plan the work, then work the plan" has become a cliche, not because it lacks wisdom but because we often do not adhere to it. I would like to alter this maxim to: "Plan the work, work the plan, then review the work rather than the plan." It's simple enough. However, it requires a willingness to go about the planning process in an integrated fashion. In other words, translate the strategic plan into shorter-term specific action plans or projects. The action plans or projects represent the "work the plan" and the plan review should concentrate on how the projects are progressing and how closely they conform to the strategies. To do that effectively, it is imperative that the action plans are presented in written form and include expected results and realistic project realization dates.

At Robin Hood Multifoods, we employ a planning process not unlike most other well-managed companies in North America. Our strategic plan has a five-year horizon and deals with:

—Which businesses the company should engage in;

—Which product lines to support with investment and which to harvest;

—What resources to allocate to which businesses;

—Product formulation and positioning;

—Competitive pricing and costs;

—Organizational structure and human resources; and

—Unit sale and profit goals.

The annually updated five-year strategic plan is the basis for the development of our one-year plan which is, in practice, a compendium of specific actions that will be taken in pursuit of the sales and profit targets set in the updated plan.

Here are some examples of the format used in shorter-term plans, dealing with cost competitiveness:

Sample Plan 1: **Cutting Cost**

Objective:	The increase in product prices must be kept to 2 percent below inflation.
Strategy:	Evaluate all cost elements for savings and improved efficiency.
Specific actions:	Acquire a higher speed labelling machine for full operation by June 1, resulting in 8 percent per case savings in labor. Hire a licensed electrician in order to reduce the cost of outside contract work by $120M per year. Negotiate an increase in the cost of packaging material of no more than 3 percent. Contract to be concluded no later than April.

A second plan is aimed at improving sales through better marketing strategies.

Plan 2: **Selling More Flour**

Objective:	Maintain market share leadership at 45 percent while also maintaining margins.
Strategy:	Convince both the consumer and the trade of our brand's consistent high quality and of our expertise in and support of "from scratch" home baking.
Actions:	Advertise in selected high-consumption areas. Execute a high-profile consumer and trade promotion during the high season for in-house baking. Maintain premium price relative to branded competition of X percent, and, to generics, of Y percent.

Other actions relevant to the execution of the strategy could be listed, but the point is that during the periodic, time-consuming plan reviews, I would focus on the specific actions rather than on the objectives and strategies.

The strategic plan is of immense importance, and significant effort must be put in to developing it. The process of executing the strategic plan is of equal importance and in terms of time and human resources requires much more than the development of the strategies. Execution commits the company to significant sums of money, and makes the sales margins and profits happen.

Evaluating a Strategy: Straight Arrows and Hockey Sticks

James R. Wessel
President, Worldwide Glove SBU
Becton Dickinson & Co.

Over the years, we've developed several ideas to help in the preliminary evaluation of a strategic plan. At Becton Dickinson, it is the division presidents' task to review the plan prior to presentation to the Corporate Strategic Review Committee. That committee has many resources at its disposal and conducts a thorough review both quantitatively and qualitatively. It is the division presidents' job to screen out major blunders before the plan reaches the review committee. That is not a simple task because the quality of a plan may not be correlated with the quality of its presentation. Bad plans can be well presented and vice-versa.

If we look at the historical performance of a key variable, a trend line can be established. The main variable can be income, number of sales, share of market, or any other important variable. It can be for a product line or for a strategic business unit. What we forecast for the future determines whether or not the strategic plan will take the direction of a "straight arrow" or a "hockey stick."

The straight arrow calls for a continuation of the current trend. In general, this type of strategic plan is much easier to evaluate. It probably calls for a continuation of current activities; it assumes that competitors will continue to behave as they have in the past; and that there are relatively few new forces in the field. While the rules for evaluation remain the same, this type of plan automatically has a higher degree of credibility than the hockey stick.

The hockey stick calls for a change in the trend line of a key variable. Normally, this is a projected increase. That characteristic up or down turn from the trend line makes the overall graph look like a hockey stick. This type of strategic plan requires more rigorous analysis.

In order to help in the evaluation of a plan, we have developed the six Cs of strategic plan evaluation. They are a reminder to consider the important factors in a strategic plan.

Customer. A successful strategic plan has a customer focus. It clearly describes customer needs and how those needs are going to to be satisfied. If this is a straight arrow plan, then the needs will be satisfied in much the same way they were in the past. A hockey stick requires a different approach.

In all good strategic plans, customer satisfaction is backed up by market research, focus groups, and interviews with the customer. In poor plans, the approach to customer satisfaction is often based only on the opinion of the strategic unit leader.

Competitor. Once we know how we're going to service the customer, then it is important to clearly understand why we are able to do this better than our competitors. Are we protected by patents or large market shares? Do we have unique capabilities in distribution or sales support? Can our competitors match or exceed our quality level? What are they likely to do in response to the initiatives described in the strategic plan?

Commitment. Developing a strategic plan idea is only the beginning. Implementation is the difficult part. It requires the commitment of a large number of individuals over a long period of time. Any good strategic plan will describe in detail how this is going to be done. It will outline staffing requirements, organization, incentive systems, and why people are going to want to succeed.

It may also describe systems for monitoring competitive reaction so the committed people can then react to sustain the advantage. It is not only essential that we determine tasks but also that we talk about who is going to do the work. Successful strategic plans are able to enlist the commitment of a large number of individuals working towards a common goal.

Clarity. If we are going to have this commitment, it is essential for the strategic plan to be clear. The underlying strategy must be simply stated so it can be understood by the people who have to make the commitment. If it requires several pages to describe a strategy, it will be impossible to communicate and difficult to enlist support.

When you look at successful companies, they all have a simple way of stating their strategy. For example, Marriott Hotels simply wants to be the best hotel for business people. It works very hard to minimize the annoyances that normally accompany business travel—check-ins, check-outs, long waits at breakfast, etc. Employees can learn this basic philosophy very quickly. Therefore, it is relatively easy to gain commitment.

Continuity. The development of a significant competitive advantage cannot be developed overnight. If it were easy to develop a competitive advantage, it would also be easy to copy it and competitors would do so. Development of a significant competitive advantage is a step-by-step, ongoing process.

Any plan that shows a single step leading to a competitive advantage and a large gain in market share is probably unrealistic. If the plan covers five years, then it must indicate how annual improvements in key variables are going to occur. These annual incremental improvements are what lead to the long-term competitive advantage and makes the strategic plan realistic.

Consistency. A strategic plan must have internal consistency. If we are forecasting an increase in sales, then it would be reasonable to expect an increase in marketing expenses, a decrease in margins, and a decrease in income. These three things would add up to internal consistency. Plans that show increasing sales, increasing margins, increasing market share, and increasing profits are internally inconsistent. You can't accomplish all simultaneously.

Evaluating strategic plans is not easy. Dedicated implementation can make a success of a mediocre plan. Lack of commitment will ensure the failure of the best. To quote Peter Drucker, "Everything eventually deteriorates into hard work." And evaluating strategic plans is no exception.

Part III
Who Owns the Plan— The Corporation vs. The SBU

Fostering Strategic Thinking Throughout the Organization

L. David Moore
President and Managing Director
Interchem, Inc.

For almost 20 years Corporate America has worshipped at the totem of "The Strategic Plan." But like a totem, most versions of the strategic plan have no life and have let many good, successful businessmen question the worth of strategic planning. And yet, I strongly believe in it, sponsor it, and accept it as a way of promoting strategic thinking throughout an organization.

Why does strategic planning often have the unintended consequence of restricting strategic thinking? I suggest the answer lies in four myths: The first myth is the belief that all you have to do is put the strategic plan in place and the business will succeed. That is wrong. Strategy is only a start in generating good business. But since it is a start, it leads to the second myth: Bottom-up strategic planning is the way to go. That is wrong, too. I have worked for a *Fortune* 100 company and a *Fortune* 300 company, and both used bottom-up strategic planning. Neither survived. They were lost because the CEO did not accept the bottom-up plan; he was either too kind or too uncommunicative to let those hard-working, bottom-up planners know his feelings. Thus the operating people were going in one direction and the CEO in another. This is exactly the problem that strategic planning is meant to overcome.

This immediately leads to the third myth: The corporate planner is the one who develops the strategic plan for the corporation. Again, wrong. Planning is so much a part of conducting business activities throughout an organization that the planner should be the head of the business unit. In the case of the corporation, the chief planning officer is the CEO, who decides which businesses the company should concentrate on, which to let slip. In the same vein, the division general manager is the chief planning officer for the division and uses planning input to manage. However, despite this line-management involvement, the strategic direction of a corporation should never be decided by the lowest managerial level, as proposed in a bottom-up approach, because that level has the least insight about anything except its own little sphere of influence. Nor should the strategic direction of the corporation be decided at the highest managerial level, because that level is often isolated and has the least solid information on unit capabilities. The best corporate strategic plan and true corporate strategic thinking comes from some ill-defined meeting place in the middle of the corporation.

Strategy and tactics are different: That is the fourth myth. Strategy is developed at one level and is put into action by supporting tactics that, in turn, become the strategy for a lower operating level. This continues throughout the organization.

These four myths, in my opinion, lead to three truths: First, the strategic plan is not business, but if it leads to strategic thinking it can be a good aid to conducting good business. Second, strategic thinking does not come from the lowest managerial level, nor does it come from the highest managerial level. Instead, strategic thinking is developed from the middle of an organization where knowledge and insight meet, hopefully in a cooperative attitude rather than in a hostile clash. Finally, there must be a cooperative dialogue, without barriers to communication. This can happen when each operating level accepts the challenge to openly communicate, using the tools generated to develop the strategic plan.

Fostering Strategic Thinking

Uniform methodology for evaluation and uniform terminology for communication must be used in order to foster strategic thinking. This uniformity should be established by someone with the title of corporate planner; but, whatever the title, he or she is not the person who does the planning. The planning is done by the line manager who is held responsible for the results of his or her business unit. If you do otherwise, strategic thinking will never occur throughout the organization.

I have been in organizations where the corporate planner established a war room once a year and came forward with a tome designated *The Strategic Plan*. When completed, that tome would be worshipped for a brief time and then would gather dust while the line managers conducted their business in their own, distinctive ways. This once-a-year war room philosophy is wasted effort and has led to a disenchantment with strategic planning and thinking and with the corporate planner on the part of many corporations.

But the corporate planner does have a necessary function to perform. He or she establishes a uniform procedure for evaluating market demands and competitive activities for all business units. It does not make sense for one business unit to label 3 percent unit growth as exploding market demand while another deems 3 percent a maintenance market demand and would define 10 percent as an exploding market. Uniform evaluation and communication techniques must be used throughout the organization, or else the effort becomes meaningless to the CEO.

The evaluative methodology must also be communicated in an easily understood way. In my opinion, this has been one of the great failures because the strategic plan has commonly become a compendium of the evaluative results for each business unit. An example of such a problem occurred at a $3 billion chemical company. It had 72 strategic business units (SBUs). The evaluative methodology for each SBU required at least 20 pages of charts, forms, and written documentation. Thus, the strategic plan consisted of over 1400 pages of data plus an executive summary written by the planning department. My guess is that the CEO would only read the summary of a few favorite SBUs and then give a sigh of relief.

In the last two companies I have been with, we have changed that approach with good results. Instead of publishing the evaluative methodology with its many forms and data, we have left that document at the SBU. We then asked each SBU to write a two- to four-page report called a strategic direction paper (SDP). In the SDP, the line manager outlines: (1) the four to six major problems and issues facing the SBU; (2) the two to four solutions evaluated to resolve each issue; (3) the chosen option in more detail; (4) the program and the capital and/or manpower needs required to follow the chosen alternative; and (5) a three- to five-year projection of the possible results if the program is followed.

Without having done the evaluation, the line manager cannot write an SDP that will stand up to scrutiny. In my case, as CEO of a $400-million business, I can easily digest the 50 to 100 pages coming from our 25 SBUs.

The "dialogue phase" is the most important. At this point, insight and information come together. The discussion is conducted by about four corporate and four to five divisional staff members. The goal for this discussion is to voice objections to concurrence with the SDP and to end up with an agreement. In managing this phase, we have found it viable to discuss the strategic direction papers for three, and possibly four, SBUs per day. Because of the SDP approach, we have been able to develop a good dialogue during which the line manager may have to refer to his or her evaluative methodology to justify his or her response to such questions as:

- Why are these major issues?
- Why was that option chosen?
- Can you really run that program with that capital or manpower input?
- How comfortable are you that the chosen programs will generate the anticipated results in the chosen time frame?

But because of the SDP approach, the corporate people do not have to evaluate reams of evaluative data unless the chosen direction doesn't make sense or the results do not seem worth the effort. In those cases, the corporate people may have to dig back into the evaluation. As another advantage, if the corporate staff cannot accept the chosen direction for all SBUs because of capital or manpower restraints, then the compendium of all SDPs contains enough data to allow the CEO to pick which SBUs to support.

If the chosen direction in the SDP is accepted, then it must be followed because the line manager has presented something based on uniform evaluation and communicated in a way that can be digested and understood. Furthermore, no additional communication on strategy is required until the next scheduled meetings on strategy. If, however, a chosen strategic direction is not followed, or another alternative is chosen, or a major issue crops up, or the competitive environment undergoes a significant change, then the SDP and the dialogue session have to be repeated no matter what time of year or what part of the normal strategic cycle must be broken into.

With one exception or shortcoming, this process has overcome many of the problems inherent in the strategic plan. The advantages are:

1) Instead of being a tome filled with indigestible data, the SDP is a useful document and an outline for a dialogue; and

2) The SDP becomes a day-to-day living document, easily changed as circumstances change but inviolate to change in the absence of major environmental changes. Thus, the SDP becomes a commitment by the line manager, whereas the strategic plan is often ignored.

Reward is the one shortcoming with this process. We are still a nation that measures success on a short-term basis, and whereas the SDP process permits personal rewards on achieving strategic objectives, human nature tends to reward the immediate profit contributor more than the successful strategist. That is still true with us, but we're working on it. When the reward system is in place, then we will be using all the elements needed to foster strategic thinking throughout the organization, including:

- Uniform methods for business evaluation;
- Uniform terms for communicating that evaluation;
- Easily digested communications based on evaluation but directed toward issues, problem solving, and anticipated results as the problems are solved;
- Open dialogue directed toward consensus for strategic direction and emphasizing where the SBU is, where it is going, and how it is going to get there;
- An ability to change strategic direction with major environmental changes whenever they may occur rather than waiting for the normal strategic planning cycle; and
- A reward system based on strategic results.

Strategic thinking is doable and can be used to chart your course, but only if it is fostered throughout the organization.

Whose Plan Is It Anyway?

S. Morgan Morton
President
Warner-Lambert Canada Inc.

As long as that question is being asked, I can guarantee there is a problem. Unfortunately, in far too many situations, general managers of divisions (subunits of large companies) find themselves having to wrestle with this problem.

As a division manager, the division's strategic plan must be yours. If you are placed in a position where you are asked, or expected, to carry out a long-range plan you don't agree with, you are headed for trouble. You really have only three options:

1. You can buy into the plan, and I mean really buy in, don't just be a good soldier. If you're nothing more than a good soldier, your subordinates are going to see right through you.

2. You can sell your management on your plan or on a plan that you believe in.

3. If you aren't able to accomplish either, I suggest that you find something else to do.

I firmly believe that the key strategic planner must be the division head. One situation that illustrates this point occurred in the mid 1970s when I was a marketing manager for a large consumer products division. The division president had unsuccessfully attempted to present a strategic plan on a specific line of business to corporate management. This division president had been told that his invest/grow plan was not acceptable and that he should manage the division's business as a follower and attempt to maintain a strong number 2 position against a very large and powerful number 1. This line of reasoning was completely alien to him. He firmly believed in being the best but was being told, for the first time, to accept being number 2 and not to attempt to become number 1 because it was too risky and could be too costly.

Three things became very clear to me at this point: First, he had gotten clear direction from corporate management as to exactly what their expectations were. Second, it was obvious that this manager was not capable of managing a business as a number 2. He did not believe in the strategy that he was expected to carry out. Third, he was venting his negative feelings to me, a subordinate and the person who was going to have the responsibility for developing the tactical application of the strategic plan.

Needless to say, it didn't work. This division president was shortly transferred to a very obvious, invest/grow business situation and, of course, this made him happy and was probably the best utilization of his talent. The marketing manager responsible for carrying out the plan was transferred within a few months to another business. New management then attempted to meet the corporate strategic objectives and within 18 months the business was driven from a strong number 2 position to an eroding number 3 position.

From my perspective, the entire plan failed because no one with day-to-day responsibility for the business understood what was to be accomplished by remaining the strong number 2 and, therefore, the organization could not respond to the challenge.

I certainly don't want to minimize the importance of corporate management's role in the success of any division manager's strategic plan. Corporate management support of any strategic program is vital. There are several other players that are important as well. In addition to corporate management, the division manager must be very cognizant of the importance of the staff executive who heads corporate planning. Also of importance are consultants, whether they are hired by the corporate staff or by the division manager. Lastly, the most important constituency of the division manager is the manager's staff; they must also buy into the plan.

In a typical long-range planning process, division personnel begin to sort out where they want to go and what they should be doing with the business. The plan is then presented as a document and goes through the various chains of command to the corporate level for approval. And corporate management will either be fully supportive, ask for slight modifications, or want to go in a completely different direction.

This seems like a very straightforward process. In many instances, however, corporate management does not give clear feedback concerning how they feel about the plan. Many times I believe this is done for purposes of safety. Corporate executives are sometimes unclear because they are unsure about the potential success of a plan. They tend to be rather unresponsive and this is probably the worst thing that can happen. Often I will inquire as to how strategic planning presentations were received by corporate management. A typical response will be, "Oh, I think it went OK. They didn't have a lot to say, but I think they bought into it."

My initial response is "watch out, something doesn't feel right." If there was a complete buy-in to the plan, the manager will know it. He can judge agreement based upon the comments; either written or oral, that will come from management at the conclusion of that presentation. You should never leave a presentation or meeting concerning your strategic plan with corporate management without a very clear understanding of whether or not they're going to give the plan full support.

This is particularly true if the plan involves a redirection of the business and requires financial support from outside the division. If you ever have any doubts as to where you stand with your boss regarding acceptance of your plan, I suggest that you develop highly focused questions designed to confirm whether or not you have support. Also, it is extremely important that the entire organization hear this support; have it backed up in writing or by other form of formal communication from corporate management.

One of the biggest assets or potential road blocks to a division manager in the strategic planning process is the executive responsible for the strategic planning at the corporate level. This individual has more clout in the process than generally given credit. In many instances, this executive has far more contact and exposure to senior executives than the person with the operating responsibility for the division. The division manager using this resource to advantage will usually be far more effective in getting corporate support than one who does not.

When I first took over the position of director of corporate planning, I sat one-on-one with each division president to find out what assistance I could give to the division: in developing the plan and in getting the plan approved at the corporate level.

In some instances, division presidents would approach me and outline what they were hoping to accomplish and ask for my perspective about whether or not their plans would be approved and financed at the corporate level. In many instances, by making suggestions modifying the plan, we were able to sell the plan and gain full support at all levels.

The role of corporate staff personnel in the successful implementation of any division's Strategic Plan is crucial. From my experience, corporate staff personnel are highly responsive to what they perceive to be the goals and objectives of senior corporate management. They will even become pro-active in looking for ways to accelerate activities and add value to many of the division's individual objectives.

In many cases, particularly where managers are looking for a significant change in direction or solutions to problem businesses, consultants will become part of the strategic planning process. The advantage of general consultants is that they have expertise that may not exist within a division and the ability to look at a business situation in a far more objective manner than those very close to it. This objectivity can be extremely important when one is attempting to sort out the strengths and weaknesses of a given business operation.

In my opinion, consultants are hired by corporate management to assist the divisions in sorting out their individual plans. Two major problems arise when this occurs: in the case of the corporate planning executive, consultants hired by corporate management are sometimes perceived as spies. Also, too often these consultants arrive, go through long periods of analysis and pursue information, and then help to develop rather grandiose plans on paper. But, before the ink is dry, they are on to their next assignment with little or no ownership of the results of the planning activity.

The best consultants in my opinion are those who act as facilitators. They assist in the organization of the process and work one-on-one with the division manager to assist in making sure that all the questions have been asked and that the manager responsible for implementing the plan has thought through the pros and cons of each of its elements. This type of consultant is extremely important.

I also believe that the direction for a business must be set by the division president, but the critical implementation of any strategic plan must be carried out by his/her staff. This staff must buy into the direction of the plan and share the vision of where the business is going and how it's going to get there.

The successful implementation of any strategic plan relies on three very important considerations: communication, communication, communication. The general manager must seize upon every opportunity to reaffirm the strategic direction of the business and articulate where the business is going and the role of each unit in carrying out specific activities related to the achievement of the overall plan.

The primary reason for strong communication is to educate. One of your objectives is to develop missionaries; you want your managers to be able to tell all of their subordinates exactly where the business is going and to explain their role in the plan. Frequent communication is also a safeguard. Today, American organizations undergo frequent personnel changes: transfers between divisions and new employees coming in due to business expansions and turnover. Frequent communication assures that the prime directive is not lost in the shuffle.

We should keep two thoughts in mind as we think about this communication process: Never lose sight of the fact that the longer-term vision of the business may be very clear to top management but for most of the organization the focus is on much shorter time frames, usually the 12-month operating plan. In any communication we want to give the long-term perspective but also to concentrate on the linkage between the current operating plan or specific projects and the longer-term plan.

Probably the most difficult task of any division general manager is sorting out the direction for the business. This is a process that should not be rushed. It requires a fair amount of analysis and thought and all the resources that can be marshaled in developing different points of view should be used. Once you have that vision and you know where you want to go, then the fun begins. If you're able to garner the support of corporate management, corporate support staffs, and your own staff, you will be well on your way to success.

Meeting Corporate *and* Divisional Planning Needs

Ronald B. Clark
Senior Partner
Mallory Associates
(Formerly President, Jaffra Cosmetics, Division of Gillette)

The Problem

Division presidents need to comply with corporate requirements for strategic information; fulfill corporate requirements for financial results; and, sometimes, to be the heroes who pick up the slack for "problem" units in their corporate group of business units. Division presidents need to create strategies that are logical for their business, to sell their teams' strategic plan to corporate management and to staffs that have their own personal interests, and to defend their divisions to corporate management and while defending the corporation and its strategies to division management. In short, a division president must be the buffer while still being the leader. All this creates a very complex role for the division president and poses a very subtle set of questions that must be answered in order to develop, sell, and maintain a successful division strategic plan.

The Solution

The division president must clearly define the need, strategy, and role of his or her division or subsidiary within the corporation and know the definition of "success" in terms of percent growth in profit, increased profit, and market share. What is the definition of success for the division within the parent corporation? Does the corporation have a fair and logical understanding of the division's strategic needs and of the division and its business? If corporate management's experience is mostly in different industries, are they accepting enough, or "too" accepting, of a division's strategies and plan? Are their goals for the division largely based on what will satisfy Wall Street or what is the industry average?

The division's clearly defined mission has to be the one sold to the division's own management. Selling this carefully weighed and agreed upon plan to the division management will probably be a more time-consuming process than selling it to the corporate management.

Process Realities

Top corporate management, like the division's president, is usually short of time. Sometimes getting approval from corporate management is "too" easy. They often have to review three or four plans per day for a week or more and, unfortunately, may accept a plan that hasn't been fully communicated, or that, due to time constraints, reflect compromise agreements that aren't good for either the division or the corporation.

The next challenge the division president must face is defending the integrity and continuity of a well-conceived, strategically sound plan against raids by the corporate home office. Corporate management will sometimes agree to a plan, its mission, and even its tactics, but later renege or "adjust" agreements, downsize resource allocations and, in effect, change the integrity of the plan. This is wrong, but happens all too often in corporations in order to meet short-term needs.

I have been on both sides of the "resource allocation" fence. As a subsidiary president, I had funds critical to the success of a strategic plan taken away after the funds were approved by the parent corporation. These approved resources were, in the minds of my key management members, the cornerstone of the plan. When I returned to explain that they were no longer available, my personal credibility, the credibility of the parent corporation, and the credibility of the whole strategic planning process suffered greatly! At this point, the division president is placed in a very difficult position. He or she can be a good soldier—which I believe is the general reaction—or choose to scream, rant, and resign. The latter doesn't happen, even though an opportunity to pursue "personal interests" sounds very attractive.

A more subtle, but no less harmful threat to a plan's integrity is "taking another look." The division president takes the plan back to his or her staff to review it in light of changing conditions. The corporate staff groups are usually as embarrassed as the division president is angry about having to go back and rethink something that everyone has already agreed to. As compromises are made on both sides, the two organizations stop communicating, begin to bicker and to hide things. What started out as a mutually agreed-upon promising future, becomes a rather unhappy, unproductive union.

The key question is: Whose plan is it? I believe that most corporate CEOs want corporate strategic planning to be in the best interest of the divisions as well as the parent company. A good CEO knows that the sum of the parts equals the total and empathizes with the division CEO's position. However, with the stratification in most U.S. multinationals today, there are a "lot of cooks tending the broth." The CEO's best intentions get involved with those of the vice chairman, the chief operating and financial officers, the group VPs, the staff VPs, ad infinitum.

In many organizations, the strategic plan is conceived by the division general manager, hopefully developed and supported by his or her management team, probably with too much involvement and the approval of the division general manager's boss and other corporate staffs. Thus, in many cases, the final strategic plan is nobody's plan. So, you see divisions being directed by a strategic plan that, instead of serving as a working "road map" ends up in the drawers of division management, to be reviewed only at next year's planning cycle. This process happens far too often in far too many organizations.

The Way It Should Be Done

It is almost a cliche to say that the division's strategic plan must be choreographed and directed by the division president, but developed by his or her functional and staff groups. These should be assisted, if needed, by corporate staffs. Resource allocation should be blessed by corporate top management. The strategic plan then becomes everybody's plan. It is the responsibility of the division president, who is the one most responsible, to make sure the plan belongs to everybody.

This creative process hopefully creates constructive controversy. Division presidents should be the defenders of the plan and the ones who attract funds away from other projects and other corporate groups. Interrelationship skills must be honed to win the resources necessary to fund the division, especially if the strategic plan takes the division's business into relatively uncharted waters.

Division presidents need to win their immediate superior's approval, and, if the corporation is very large and the division important to overall corporate strategy, they must also win the approval of a number of bosses and their staffs. Division presidents, especially those with higher corporate aspirations, have to put their careers on the line during the strategic planning process and risk losing the support of corporate top management and possibly creating negative scenarios: If a division president goes against corporate top management but gets their approval, and then proves to have been right, he can be a hero, depending on how objective and broad-minded corporate management is. If he or she is proven wrong, the next step is to get the resume updated. On the other hand, being more conciliatory and losing the battle can result in a loss of credibility with top corporate management. Even more seriously, too much acquiescence can create a loss of credibility with one's own staff. If the results are good, the division president will probably survive. If not, he or she may lose the battle and the war.

The division president's role is very delicate. It can create high career risks, as well as risks for the entire division's management group and the division itself. It must be carefully assessed. Such risks go with the turf of being president of a subsidiary or division. If the division president doesn't assume the risks inherent in the creation, development, and execution of the strategic plan, the division will be run by that infamous group, "they." And they can't strategically manage the division; that has to be done, ultimately, by one person—the division general manager.

Corporate management should establish an environment of mutual respect so the division president can develop and execute plans properly. Coaching from the top can be very important, but usurping authority from division management only causes the creation of poorly supported strategies. Corporate top management must give the division general manager the chance to win the game.

Accommodating Different Businesses With One Planning System

D. Kent Tippy
Vice President, Soabar Products Group
Avery International

Can a single strategic planning system be all things to all businesses regardless of their type or market situation? Those of you who have responsibility for managing a number of different strategic business units (SBUs), or have an overall planning role, must have faced this perplexing issue more than once.

I've been faced with this issue both as a line manager and as a corporate planner. Consider the following three businesses, all part of the same corporation and in need of a strategic plan:

The first is a consumer product business growing in excess of 20 percent per year. It enjoys almost 70 percent market share and very high margins as a result of a large price umbrella and a growing marketplace.

The second is an industrially oriented, small machine business, which after a history of good performance has begun to stagger. Costs and profits are going in the opposite direction. The market is changing to a new technology and the business is saddled with outmoded manufacturing methods and equipment.

The third business is quite different. It involves a fledgling, high-tech joint venture with a company many times its size. The technological feasibility is not completely proven, the market does not yet exist, the risks are not completely understood, and the price tag is quite large. However, even a conservative estimate of sales and profits causes the heart to flutter.

Should these three businesses plan strategies in the same manner using the same system? How can a single planning system meet the needs of all, and what modifications need to be made for the system to be productive for everyone, corporate and operating unit alike?

Why not just let them do what they want? Why have a single planning system in the first place? Well, an officially anointed system is needed if for no other reason than to provide the line manager with a set of expectations for the desired results. A system helps provide a road map. It acts as a guide. This is important since planning in a multi-SBU environment is not an isolated exercise—planning-wise, everyone should operate in the same culture. Also, without it, the corporate office has little chance to read, assimilate, and engage in critical feedback with the planning unit.

At my company, we have over 40 separate business units that develop plans. Without some commonality of approach, the process would be unmanageable and worthless. A good planning system is appropriate and has value for all businesses, regardless of type. But what are the characteristics and elements of a good planning system?

I think the aspect that breathes life into a system is the active participation of the top managers or CEO. Strategic planning done by the planning officer alone is generally ineffective and often ignored by the people who have to realize the plans. This has to be a dynamic process, marked by continuous, productive iterations. I'm in favor of doing strategic planning in sequential phases. This allows for more give and take, agreeing on problems or opportunities and issues, before a particular alternative is developed and incorporated into an implementation plan.

A system has to encourage "strategic" thinking and "risk of thought." After all, the whole purpose of the process is to examine where you are and what you are doing relative to the marketplace and competitors, and to ask, "What should I be doing differently?" That requires daring to take some risks in thinking of alternative courses of action. Nothing should be "unthinkable" at this stage. An interesting exercise might be to list all the alternative courses of action you can think of for taking business away from your competitor.

I also believe that strategic planning, at least during the first phase of determining issues, objectives, and directions, is a top management responsibility, not a bottom-up process. The general manager is responsible at the unit level and the CEO is responsible at the corporate level.

Brevity is paramount. Strategic plans should basically deal with "what," rather than "how." For instance, I ask my managers to summarize a plan in three to four pages, no more. If they can't do it, it is clearly too complicated, or they didn't understand it in the first place. On the other hand, while the issues and strategies need to be simply stated, they have to be based on a fair amount of quantitative and competitive analysis and analytical rigor. The most elegant strategy for the future, when based on faulty data or unreliable information, is doomed. No shortcuts here.

The right balance of responsibility between the corporate planner and the business unit is crucial. The strategic planning process needs to be operationally led, with corporate involvement and interaction. The corporate planner should provide a method for carrying out the plan and act as a counselor and advisor—someone with whom ideas can be discussed.

The Elements of a Successful Planning System

My feeling is that there is too much mystery surrounding strategic planning. It is a fairly straightforward process but that's not to say it's easy. Arriving at creative strategies can be difficult and implementing the plan certainly arduous but following the plan should not be complex.

In my experience, both as a planning practitioner and administrator, these elements are key: First, identify the SBU for which a plan should be developed.

Is it a group of products or the whole division? It's not always obvious. An SBU has to be measurable and separate enough so action can be taken directly to affect it. Second, a successful planning process is always external in focus. Remember, the goal of this exercise is to examine what you are doing in relation to the marketplace, what your competitors are doing, and to see if there are alternative ways to accomplish your objective, which is beating your competition. Third, identify your competitive strengths and weaknesses in the market place; plus the direction and size of that market. External factors, such as governmental regulations, should also be listed and assessed.

Next come the objective statements that deal with key strategic issues. They set the stage for everything that comes thereafter. For example:

> "How can Cheerios breakfast cereal increase market share to become the leading brand ahead of Kelloggs Corn Flakes by 1993?" The objective is short, succinct, understandable.
>
> "How can we lower manufacturing costs and operating expenses to become the low-cost producer?"

The next step is to list alternative ways to strategically deal with each critical issue. In the Cheerios/Kelloggs Corn Flakes example, what might be some alternatives ways for Cheerios to increase share?

- Infesting the corn crop (fairly dramatic);
- Slashing price by 25 percent (may make boss nervous);
- Reformulating the product (better taste);
- A new product position (the "healthy" alternative)
- Developing a secondary-usage profile (like Arm'n Hammer baking soda)
- Developing companion product—a "flanker" product

The last alternative is exactly what was done—a new product called Honey Nut Cheerios was developed that enlarged Cheerios' market share to the point of achieving, at least back in 1980, the number 1 brand position.

After the possible alternative strategies are identified, developing first-cut resource requirements, including capital, people, etc. is the next step; it leads to a set of preliminary financial outcomes.

Then it's time to get the corporate level involved. It's time to discuss the alternatives with them—to allow for input and to make sure the alternative strategy selected is acceptable before the implementation plan is developed.

Be it Kelloggs fending off upstarts for the number 1 position in cereal; a regulated utility trying to raise money to build new low-cost plants; or an automotive company trying to survive the onslaught of foreign competition and cut costs at the same time, these elements are the guts of any successful planning system. Then there is the fledgling, high-tech, joint venture example: Does our single system apply here, too? Well, yes and no. It can, but ventures like this are generally held outside the formal planning system since they seem to be constantly planning, changing, and replanning.

The point is that there are certainly exceptions to "one system fits all" thinking. And there should be; systems can't be sacrosanct. Strict adherence to any system can be deadly if it gets in the way of creativity. After all, it is the processes and results that are important, not the system. So flexibility has to be part of the planning culture. If a particular section or format doesn't work for you, change it.

What other accommodations make sense? How often should an SBU do a plan? Conventional wisdom says every year. But I honestly believe that there are times when nothing has really changed for a business. So I also believe in long- and short-form methodologies. Businesses are encouraged to develop a "short-form" plan if they did not experience a change in marketplace conditions, or a new competitive threat or change in competitors' strategy, or a change in the basic underlying cost mechanics or in technology and are not proposing a new strategy. The purpose of which is to verify and update the current plan and information.

Strategic planning is no mystery. It should have a set of fairly straightforward data requirements that lead to some key issues and alternative courses of action. It has to be driven by the top guy, and be more top down than bottom up. The SBU has to do the plan. And it has to be flexible—not only the system but the people involved. It has to be marketplace, externally oriented—and it shouldn't be overly long or complicated. If we can accomplish all this, then our Mr. Caslow here may be in a better position to respond.

"You know what I'd like to do, Caslow? I'd like to create a far-reaching, innovative program that will open a lot of channels, offer great opportunities, link up with all kinds of things, and enable something or other to happen. Any ideas?"

Part IV
Making It Work in the Marketplace

The Incremental Approach to Strategic Planning

Vincent A. Calarco
Chairman, President and Chief Executive Officer
Crompton & Knowles Corporation

Over the years and through several economic cycles, experience has taught me that we derive the best value from strategic planning if we adhere to five important guidelines.

First, the basis of strategic planning is strategic thinking. Your managers should be thinking of the long-range strategic impact of their decisions as well as the day-to-day consequences. Thinking strategically leads naturally to strategic management.

Second, planning begins when your senior executives have a clear and precise concept of your company's direction, which they then convey to your managers.

Third, planning should be integrated into the job responsibilities of the line managers. Since they are closest to your markets and customers, their input is vital to a plan's successful execution.

Fourth, planning is an ongoing process, not an end. Plans should be altered if obstacles are encountered.

Fifth, planning should be broken down into incremental steps. There should be specific mileposts toward achieving the plan's goal, and progress toward meeting those mileposts should be regularly evaluated. This assessment process helps identify the plan's cost effectiveness.

At Crompton & Knowles, we measure the results of strategic planning and its relevance to our markets, we determine whether it is cost effective, and how it's been an aid to our progress. And we see it as a roadmap for reaching our ultimate objective—winning.

The roadmap for strategic planning begins with an identification of businesses, technologies, and markets that a company should try to develop to create long-term value. It starts with two key questions: "What's our business now? What should it be?" Those questions may seem self-evident, but if they are seriously discussed and candidly answered, they can help you decide if your planning process is grounded in the reality of your business. They're the first check on whether strategic planning is relevant to the demands of your markets.

When you ask these questions, you are stepping outside the box of your regular day-to-day operations and looking at them from a different perspective. You are searching for the market niches that you may have overlooked and for anything else that could improve your business. Essentially, you are seeking major breakthroughs that will enhance your profitability.

The first person to ask these questions is the chief executive officer. At Crompton & Knowles, we don't have a separate corporate planning department, so if anyone could be considered the director of planning, it would be me as the CEO. If I am the director of strategic planning, then all of our senior operating managers constitute our planning staff. The formation, development, and implementation of our strategic plans are integral to the responsibilities of our executives. They participate in the planning process from the very beginning. Our plans have worked best when we've limited the organizational separation between myself as chief planner and the managers who develop and execute the plans.

We're so convinced that responsibility for planning should be spread throughout the organization that we've made it a measure of performance. Our Management Incentive Plan ties a manager's compensation, including such indirect compensation as stock options, to how well he or she develops and executes strategic plans. Needless to say, our people work very hard at thinking and then at planning and managing strategically.

I think recent business history provides ample evidence that involving line managers in planning keeps them grounded in the fundamentals of your markets so that you don't become lost in the planning process itself or in data that are not pertinent. If planning works best when it is the responsibility of managers at all levels, the next question is: How should it be integrated throughout management? And how do chief executives and senior managers communicate a clear and precise idea of their company's direction to the rest of the management team? This requires, for want of a better word, as much planning and careful implementation as strategic plans themselves.

First of all, planning cannot be vague and amorphous, or seen as a magic formula for success. You won't have a successful corporate-wide planning process if you set vague goals, such as, "increase earnings," or "grow market share," or "develop new markets." Not only will people not know where to go, but they may march off in opposite directions.

Consider, for example, the goal of "improving the bottom line." To an accountant, that might translate into reducing expenses by laying off employees. To a sales manager, that might translate into hiring more salespeople so a company can penetrate new markets and improve its bottom line through higher sales.

To avoid this, Crompton & Knowles takes an "incremental" approach to planning. Incremental planning extends well beyond setting specific goals. It includes the establishment of mileposts toward reaching the goal and the specific dates on which those mileposts must be reached and makes clear who is responsible and accountable for achieving them.

Breaking a plan down into incremental steps also gives us a tool for determining its cost effectiveness. We develop a cost for meeting each key part of the plan. This allows us to see if costs, such as investments in research, manufacturing capacity, or marketing, will either negate or substantially reduce the rewards that will be realized once the plan is fulfilled. We also assign responsibilities to managers within the divisions and departments affected by the plan. We make them responsible for implementing their part of the plan and give them clear reporting assignments. These are set while we are developing the plan so there is no time lapse between its formation and implementation. Each manager knows what mileposts he or she must meet and when. We follow up at regular meetings where all those responsible report on the progress they have made on achieving their goals.

This tells us how well a plan is being implemented and if changes are required. If a milepost is missed, we can correct it immediately. We can also easily determine whether our plan is realistic and succeeding, or failing. Strategy is a living guide to help us around obstacles. If we fail along the way, we change our plans and alter course.

Five years ago we devised a plan that has essentially redesigned our Davis-Standard plastics extrusion business. Step by step, we evolved a business that was primarily based on manufacturing into one that is now heavily service oriented. We began this transformation at review sessions that closely examined current market conditions. From the information that our marketing staff, sales people, and customers provided, we realized that market demand for plastics extrusion equipment was flattening. We had been improving productivity so much that our customers didn't need to order new equipment to meet rising demand. Furthermore, the plastics extrusion industry—like so many other industries—was facing a threat of increased offshore competition.

If we were to cope with these new conditions, we could no longer conduct business as usual. What we did was to look at our business and industry from the outside. From this new perspective, we decided to adopt a different approach to the plastics extrusion business. Where our business had once been built solely on making quality equipment, we would now seize the opportunity to expand into components and service as well. These new directions would enable us to increase both our market share and our overall profitability.

We began by acquiring the HES company, which was a manufacturer of electronic control equipment. This had two effects. It opened new markets for us, such as the printing industry, and it enabled us to expand our product offerings to our existing customers. They could come to us for both the extrusion and the control equipment. As a further advantage, the electronic process equipment market was somewhat more immune to foreign competition.

In an important second step, we began to emphasize after-market service. By transferring responsibilities and shifting a few key people into new assignments, we increased the size of our field service staff. We provided both our existing and new customers with services of all sorts, from repairing and rebuilding equipment to modernizing and installing it. Where once we had serviced only our own equipment, we began to offer our full line of services on other brands.

The combination of the new electronic controls business and the expanded service operation gave us an important competitive edge in dealing with the marketplace. We became a single source for all of our customers' needs. Because they could come to us for all their products and services, they were willing to pay our price for both.

As a result, over the past five years our Davis-Standard operation has outperformed its competition. Its share of the market for new extrusion equipment has increased by about five percentage points, which is excellent when you consider that this is a down market industry-wide. Over the same time period, the sales of the equipment and controls business have increased five fold. Revenues of the service business, which didn't exist five years ago, now account for almost 15 percent of our specialty process equipment and controls business.

This is the type of breakthrough success that we were seeking when we developed a new strategy for our specialty process equipment and controls business. Given the improvements in market share and sales, I think it's easy to conclude that this new strategy worked very well. Of course, I'm only relating successes—and not all of our programs have been stellar performers. But we found that failures occurred most often when we were trying to go beyond our technological and marketing expertise and what we know best.

Another example. In 1986, we divested our Kem cleaning products business. Divestments may not seem like a sterling example of a success, but the judicious pruning of a corporation is necessary for continued profitability and for establishing a basis for shareholder value. Our sale of Kem clearly illustrates the value that can be derived from the careful review of a business, its strategic importance to the company, and the cost effectiveness of various strategic alternatives.

Kem produced and distributed about 250 different cleaning, maintenance, and sanitation compounds for industrial, institutional, and commercial customers. Its market stretched from North America through Central America and the Caribbean to Europe. Sixty percent of its sales were offshore, and a costly direct sales force was employed to sell its products.

Crompton & Knowles acquired Kem in 1976 and went through several management changes in an effort to turn it around. Kem posed two basic problems for us—it was impossible to attain a competitive edge in its markets and its profitability was marginal, at best. Unlike our other two major businesses, Kem did not produce the type of value-added products and services that contributed to our profitability. As such, it did not fit into our capabilities and our strategic direction. Kem was also draining away assets and investments that could be better spent on our core businesses.

We decided in 1986 that the situation could not be rectified and began looking for a purchaser. After analyzing the situation, we found that we would realize a better value if we sold Kem piecemeal rather than as a single unit. Kem was subsequently sold in five separate transactions. We also acted directly with the buyers, and did not retain an investment banker as an intermediary. Obviously, this also added to our return.

A few clear lessons can be drawn from the successes and failures that we've realized through our incremental approach to strategic planning. First of all, we respond to market conditions because the people who are closest to the marketplace help to shape our thinking. Consequently, you know before a plan is implemented whether it will be relevant to the needs of the marketplace and represent a creative solution to a customer's problems.

Secondly, because we have separated the planning process into incremental steps, we can identify whether the strategy is being executed according to our plan. Corrective action can be taken quickly, and we don't have to wait until the plan is in place before we identify problems. Our managers know where all the pieces of a plan are and how they fit together. They can focus on keeping all the pieces moving in the right direction on the right timetable.

Thirdly, it is easy to determine cost-effectiveness with this approach to planning because you can measure the cost of implementing each step of a plan against its reward. You are also spared the cost of failure as measured in lost sales, scrapped production plans, and factories that have to be retooled to manufacture products to replace the ones that won't sell.

There's really no great magic to it. Effective planning programs require the same painstaking, incremental approach to detail that all successful business actions require. This approach is summarized in these nine points:

- Define your plan's objectives;
- Quantify them;
- Consider alternatives;
- Evaluate the cost-effectiveness of each alternative;
- Decide on a course of action;
- Develop incremental plans, with costs, to achieve your overall goal;
- Monitor and follow up the implementation of your plan;
- Change as necessary;
- And, win.

Implementing Strategy: Commitment Without a Straight Jacket

Ellen M. Hancock
Vice President & General Manager, Communication Systems
IBM

To me, strategic planning is not just making things happen, it's making things happen at the right time, for the right reasons, and in a way that makes logical, efficient, and maximum use of all the skills and experience available. It is one of the tools that a decision maker must have. It sets the basis, the rationale, and the priorities for the actions that follow.

Obviously, then, planners must be in tune with every internal and external aspect of the business. And they must be able to respond and adjust whenever events occur that affect current operations. Strategic thinking involves thorough consideration of customer needs based on direct and candid talks with large numbers of customers.

There was a time at IBM when strategic planning was a more formalized and extensive process, involving much discussion and lengthy negotiations. Moreover, the plan required review and acceptance by the highest levels of the corporation. We relied on marketing to tell the manufacturing and development organizations the products and quantities to make. Then, manufacturing and development would gear their operations accordingly.

That worked adequately in a more leisurely time. But IBM is always looking to improve its procedures, and, as the industry heated up, as technology, customer demands, and competition moved at a faster pace, it became apparent that planning had to be more responsive to change and that constant input was required from all sources. IBM responded with two significant changes designed to bring planning and decision making down to a level closer to the customer.

The first change took place several years ago. It made product managers directly responsible for gauging marketplace needs instead of relying only on marketing strategy. It was a simple yet significant change, but it gave the product manager the independence and authority needed to develop a plan for his or her specific product. Product managers became fully responsible for developing and executing a product plan. The product manager, in effect, runs a business. And as such, wields a great deal of influence on any matter that may have an impact on his or her area of responsibility.

IBM's second change occurred in January 1988. It was a reorganization of its development and manufacturing operations into line-of-business segments.

This squarely puts decision-making responsibility in the hands of the line-of-business general managers, and gives them the authority and freedom to seize opportunities and make trade-offs in the marketplace in order to get the job done. Of course, procedures are in place to provide for communication between business units so that each one knows what the other is planning and has a chance to make comments and suggestions.

Turning Plans into Profits

When you've spent any time in the world of business, you know that the process of turning good ideas into good products is not a magical one. One recent example of this process is our introduction of two software products: Netview and Netview/PC. Both of them anticipated a quickly growing customer need and, as a result, both have been well received in the marketplace. In addition, other manufacturers are now adapting their products for attachment to them.

IBM, like several other companies, sells software that helps customers manage computer networks. These telecommunications networks connect desks in a department or sites around the world. At the technical level, network management is a housekeeping function. It keeps the information highway in good repair, watches over the quality of connecting routes, sounds the alarm if a route fails, and automatically switches to a back-up circuit if it has to. Netview tackles complexity by combining many different IBM programs into one coherent package. Netview/PC collects information from a range of IBM and non-IBM systems and devices and feeds it to Netview.

Ten years ago computer communication networks were in their infancy. Banks and airlines, for example, were distributing their workstations and printers to points far from the host computer to make reservations and deposits. Soon, various other enterprises began to develop their own extensive networks for sending information, but keeping everything straight was a real challenge.

With growth like this, we started to develop our network management software. Obviously, there was a lot more housework to keep up with. What's more, customers were finding that the network itself made important contributions to efficiency and savings. In the late 1970s and early 1980s, we answered the call for networking tools with a number of programs. They worked fine, and customers were happy. But soon, software limited to specific tasks became inadequate for the huge networks our customers were building. Network management had arrived, and customers were asking us to give them a way to simplify the management task.

How We Did It

First, we zeroed in on what our customers wanted precisely. We found three common threads. The first two called for reducing complexity:

- Networks and network management products that were easier to use;

• An approach that integrated all the various network management products;

• And a single way to manage a network of both IBM and non-IBM equipment.

These requirements were integrated into our existing strategy. Our development and marketing staffs presented their respective views and reached a consensus to further develop the strategy and fully address the customer requirements. Only after we all had agreed on a common plan did we make a commitment. Then, taking it from strategy to products was remarkably smooth. We already had a comprehensive product ready to repackage, and we were able to lead the industry with the results.

Today, our customer requirements are changing. Customers know more about computers and not only want speed but also availability and flexibility. They are better able to articulate their needs, and, as a result, we've become more market and technology driven, as we believe it should be.

Development Cycle: Netview

Our product development team, chiefly programming managers from our group's North Carolina laboratory, had had enough customer contact to clearly understand customer requirements. Our marketing forces educated by their day-to-day contact with our customers also provided information to the development team. As a result, that team knew it had to unify IBM's existing program products for network management. For example, the display screen and the various keys on the keyboard had to look and act the same from one program to the next.

First, we assigned a product manager to lay the initial groundwork. He and his team, mostly programmers who would write the actual code, test the results, and write the manuals, suggested that we take five different existing products and pull them together into a single package. The development team reviewed their work after design, code development, functional testing and system test. Then, we asked our "human factors" experts and our customers to assess Netview—the prototype and the real thing.

Naming the system was also a challenge. We needed a name that would suggest something user friendly and communicate what the system does. "Netview" filled all our requirements. There were some mixed feelings; some thought the name was too frivolous for something so important. But when we tested the name at presentations and with various marketing executives, it caught on. The naming process aside, the development of Netview took about two years from inception to final realization in 1986.

Netview/PC

Netview consolidated functions for the IBM network but we had to open it up to non-IBM devices as well. The development manager in our programming lab had the idea of a network management workstation that consolidated our various software programs into a single terminal. He wanted to put the power of the PC to work in small office environments with equipment that does not run on our mainframe architecture. He and his team were able to add that function to Netview and reuse the same software technology. But at the same time, we began to hear specific requests for different functions from our users. To fulfill those requests, we undertook an exploratory look at Netview/PC, which got underway in the summer of 1982. It showed a lot of merit and in 1983, we funded it as a strategic product. Four years later, we announced it.

Netview/PC stayed the same conceptually from start to finish. But our strategy changed during that time. For example, a great number of our customers were asking us to support products from other companies and our marketing organization agreed because it simply made good business sense.

Remember, we knew Netview was going to change the shape of our network management products, it was possible to develop the network management station to mesh with it seamlessly. We called the product Netview/PC because we made our own PC XT and PC AT the workstation for feeding information to Netview.

As soon as we decided to open up, we asked manufacturers to become involved. We saw their involvement as a major new requirement in order to raise the considerable resources that the program would require. Meanwhile, the vendors saw involvement as a chance to strengthen the appeal of their applications by linking them to the IBM name. Netview and Netview/PC were at the very heart of our overall networking strategy. Our marketing people were well aware of that and they wanted to give the products their due. The marketing team developed its plans for presenting the products in understandable terms through the press, consultants, and especially through account teams in our branch offices.

At the end of last year, just six months after first shipment, there were over 30 vendors who had announced applications or their intent to develop product applications. Our strategy paid off. Now, we're continuing to develop our Netview family by adding new functions and applications. We have a solid base to build on and a coherent, consistent and unified approach to network management.

For the Future . . .

We already know that customers will be looking for more economical ways to manage their networks, so we're making that a part of our strategy. It's important to base our product development on a strategy that's sound and reliable. I'm confident that we can trust our strategy because it's built on the needs of our customers.

Using Action Programs To Link Strategy To Implementation

Paul B. Markovits
President
Avon Direct Selling, U.S. Division
Avon Products, Inc.

Avon was founded in 1886 by an entrepreneur who had the radical idea of selling cosmetics door to door—and the even more radical idea of providing women with the opportunity to make money. That was 34 years before women could even vote. The company grew steadily for many years. By 1972, sales were more than $1 billion. But by that same year, Avon's Golden Age for Avon began to fade. Internal controls were becoming inadequate to handle what had grown into a large and complex, international operation.

Meanwhile, forces were at work in the marketplace that were destined to have a devastating effect on Avon's business. One of them was the women's movement. From 1975 to 1985, more than 12 and one-half million women entered the workforce. As a result; there were fewer women at home to recruit as representatives and fewer women at home for representatives to call on. Also, there was a growing diversity of tastes in an increasingly affluent population. Consumers wanted products suited to their differing lifestyles. The homogeneous market we had served so successfully for so many years was disappearing. Avon had to change to survive.

In late 1983, Avon was a 97-year-old company that had never had a strategic plan. We had serious problems. We knew we needed to make changes and develop a plan, but we didn't know how to go about it. That was Avon in 1983. By the end of 1986, we had a plan and were far along in the implementation process through action programs.

The plan we developed early in 1984 had three phases. The first stressed restructuring the company for increased profit and included a dramatic downsizing, a reorganization of the marketing department along brand-management lines, and a decentralization of Avon's domestic and international operations. The second phase, which began in 1985, called for investing much of the savings from phase one in consumer need-oriented marketing and sales programs. The third phase, begun in 1986 and still in effect, entails developing increasingly sophisticated systems to help us update our methods of selling and our product offerings.

In the last four years, we have repositioned Avon, a direct sales-driven company, to a contemporary provider of beauty products targeted to satisfying customers' needs for products and services. Now let's look at the planning process responsible for all these strategies.

Our strategic planning process has been very useful for senior management and for planners, but has not been very practical in terms of involving the middle managers. So, except for the most formal translations, we use an abbreviated version that we call the logic loop (see chart below). It includes the basic steps of strategic thinking:

- A situation analysis with an assessment of strengths and limitations, opportunities and threats;
- The setting of objectives;
- The development and evaluation of alternative courses of action and tactics;
- Strategic implementation programs; and
- Contingency plans.

The logic loop has proved an invaluable tool for bringing managers throughout the organization into the process of planning and implementation.

The implementation step is the key to the success of our strategic plan. For every strategy, there is a Strategic Implementation Program, which is headed by a strategy leader—someone who accepts the responsibility of leading the project to fruition. The program consists of eight steps:

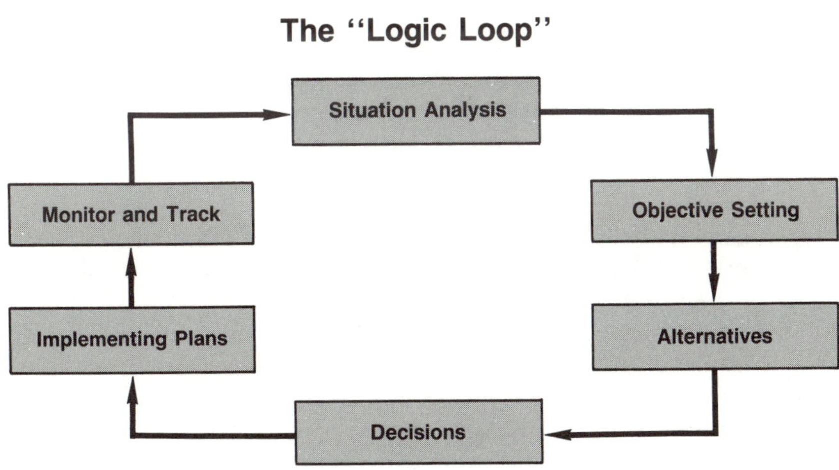

(1) Detailing the steps necessary to support the strategy;

(2) Assigning responsibility for each step;

(3) Specifying the time frame—the date each action step will be started and completed;

(4) Quantifying the resources needed—the money and the people—to implement the plan;

(5) Identifying the coordination required between different parts of the organization to implement the strategy;

(6) Establishing a plan to monitor the implementation and make sure it's effective;

(7) Determining how to communicate the successes or failures to all parties involved;

(8) Determining the circumstances under which contingency plans would be required—and whose responsibility it would be to take action if there's a deviation from the plan.

Each of those steps is taken as we begin to implement any major strategy. Possibly the most important tool to ensure that all happens as planned is what we call the Strategic Contract. This is simply an employee commitment to carry out his or her part of the program. And since we are a decentralized company, the commitments come mostly from the middle management level because they are responsible for decision making and implementation.

Our recent development and introduction of a new line of color cosmetics is a good example of this process. Color cosmetics are the most common beauty products, used by 95 percent of all women over age 15. They're also what consumers most clearly associate with Avon. But our market share had been declining since 1980.

Avon's first step was market research—the most massive single research project in our history. We spent about $1 million to measure the behavior and needs of users of makeup—to find out the why's, not just the what's. We learned, among other things, that consumers purchase products based on their commitment to a shade. They're more loyal to a color they like than to a brand. But they have great difficulty coordinating shades for lips, nails, eyes, and cheeks.

That was good news. It meant that no single brand owned the color cosmetics' category and that there was room for Avon to satisfy all of a consumer's makeup needs. But we had to completely rethink our traditional approach and to develop a more contemporary, fashionable line of color cosmetics.

Our strategy: develop a fully coordinated color line to satisfy the unique needs of each customer. To implement it, we set up a team composed of people from each of the key functional areas. We appointed a team leader, our group product director of color cosmetics, and she directed the overall project. Working with her were two teams, one for product development and one for product launch.

The product development team consisted of managers from marketing, research and development, design, purchasing, manufacturing, and cost, along with one outside consultant. Joining the product launch team were managers from marketing, merchandising and incentives, advertising, sales meetings, sales training, public relations, field communications, field sales, plus a representative from our advertising agency.

The team then proceeded with the eight steps of our Strategic Implementation Plan:

- Set objectives for market share and profitability.

- Develop a specific strategy for ensuring that these new products would satisfy consumer wants and needs. Since our research had indicated that consumers had trouble selecting and coordinating colors, we set out to develop a new color system that would allow the consumer to choose exactly what's right for her.

- Develop the product line. This activity began with an exhaustive review of our cosmetics' line, product by product, by members of the product development team. Then the R&D people on the team worked with our scientists to develop proprietary technology for creating an entirely new set of cosmetic colors. R&D tested the new products against the "old" products and competitive brands to make sure that they met key consumer needs. They also tested the products on skin to be sure they performed as positioned.

The result was a total of more that 350 shades. We grouped them into four color groups—warm, ultra warm, cool, and ultra cool—and began working on color charts and promotional materials to assist consumers in selecting the correct coordinated colors for them.

At the same time, we were also concerned with the resources needed to implement the plan, the coordination required between different parts of the organization, and how to monitor the effectiveness of the implementation program. Regarding resources, manufacturing had to know just what was involved in order to make the new products. Marketing had to develop a pricing strategy. This involved the orchestration of advertising, promotion, sales, and training—efforts that resembled preparations for D Day. In a project of this size, with so many elements, the confusion can be compounded beyond measure. The team leader served as the clearinghouse for the entire project. Otherwise, little by little, it could have drifted out of control.

The seventh part of our Strategic Implementation Plan was to communicate the results to all parties. The team leader accomplished this by having monthly meetings so that key players could review progress in detail and provide regular presentations to keep top management informed. The eighth part of the plan—contingency planning—began shortly before the launch of the new product line.

These steps are only the barest outline of our project. There were, of course, alternative strategies if needed, intricate details concerning packaging, working with vendors, and developing related strategies for different skin tones. Because of strategic planning, thinking, and implementation, in about a year and a half we created and produced a new line of cosmetics of exceptionally high quality at affordable prices. It's an industry first, and the bottom line is that our customers are applauding our efforts with their hard-earned dollars. Our cosmetics sales during the launch campaigns are up around 30 percent over the prior year—and building.

Part V
Strategy and International Considerations

Going Global

Warren J. Keegan
President
Warren J. Keegan Associates

The global corporation has evolved and its strategy agenda has shifted dramatically since the early 1960s. At that time, the emphasis was on recognizing and dealing with the differences in corporate cultures that exist in markets around the world. Today, however, since almost 50 percent of all economic activity is international, the agenda for most domestic companies calls for adopting a global stragegy. The basic approach for an "international" company is an extension strategy, whereby the firm develops a product for the home market and extends into worldwide target markets. I call this a Stage-One International Company. Most companies I know started out with this fundamental strategy.

Stage I—A Domestic Focus

A typical stage-one company is domestic in its focus, vision, and orientation. It may be local, regional, or national in its geographic scope, but its strategy is focused on domestic markets, suppliers, and competitors and its environmental information scanning is limited to the domestic market. The unconscious motto of a stage-one company: "If it's not happening in the home country, it's not happening." The world's graveyard of defunct companies is littered with stage-one companies that were sunk by the "Titanic syndrome": the often unconscious belief that they were invincible on their own turf.

The pure stage-one company is not conscious of its domestic orientation. The company operates domestically because it never considers the alternative of going international. The growing stage-one company will, when it reaches growth limits in its primary market, diversify into new markets, products, and technologies instead of focusing on penetrating international markets.

Which is better? That, of course, is impossible to say, but it is a serious mistake for any company to not consider international as opposed to market or product diversification. Harley Davidson Inc. is an example of a company that sought growth through home country diversification into such different fields as defense production and four-wheel recreational vehicles. Meanwhile, Harley's greatest strength has always been the motorcycle enthusiast market for large, expensive bikes. Although Harley's strength in this market is still largely concentrated in the United States (almost 90 percent of sales), the company realized that there is a global, luxury-priced enthusiast market and that the best opportunity for achieving a competitive advantage was to consciously and aggressively go after this market. Today, Harley is beginning to focus upon global market opportunities in its primary motorcycle market.

Stage II—An International Outlook

When a company decides to pursue opportunities outside the home country it has evolved into the stage-two category, but remains ethnocentric or home country oriented. The ethnocentric company unconsciously operates on the assumption that home country markets, methods, approaches, people, practices, and values are superior to those found elsewhere in the world. The focus of the stage-two company is on the home country market.

Because there are few, if any, people in the stage two company with international experience, it typically relies on an international division structure where people with international interest and experience can be grouped to focus on international opportunities. The marketing strategy of the stage-two company is to extend products, advertising, promotion, pricing, etc., designed for the home country market into markets around the world.

Almost every company begins its global development as a stage-two international company. It is a natural progression. Given limited resources and experience, companies must focus on what they do best. In going international, it makes sense at the beginning for companies to extend as much of the marketing mix (product, prices, promotion, and place or channels of distribution) as possible so that they can focus on how to do business in foreign countries.

A fundamental strategic maxim is that it is a mistake to attempt to simultaneously diversify into new customer *and* new product/technology markets. The international strategist observes this maxim by holding the marketing mix constant while adding new geographic or country markets. The focus of the international company is on extending the home country marketing mix and business model.

Stage III—Going Multinational

In time, the stage-two company discovers that differences in markets around the world demand an adaptation of its marketing mix in order to succeed. Toyota, for example, discovered the former when it entered the U.S. market in 1957 with its *Toyopet*. The cars were not a big hit: Critics said they were "overpriced, underpowered, and built like tanks." The car was so unsuited for the U.S. market that unsold models were shipped back to Japan. The market rejection of the Japanese *Toyopet* was chalked up by Toyota as a learning experience and a source of invaluable intelligence about market preferences. Note that Toyota did *not* define the experience as a failure. There is, for the emerging global company, no such thing as failure: only learning experiences and success in the constantly evolving strategy and experience of the company.

When a company decides to respond to market differences it evolves into a stage-three multinational that pursues a multi-domestic strategy. The focus of this company is multinational or multidomestic (as opposed to home country) and its orientation is polycentric, which assumes that markets and ways of doing business around the world are so unique that the only way to succeed internationally is to adapt to the different aspects of each national market. Like the stage-two international, the stage-three multinational, polycentric company is also predictable. In stage-three companies, each foreign subsidiary is managed as if it were an independent city state. The subsidiaries are part of an area structure in which each country is part of a regional organization that reports to world headquarters. The stage-three marketing strategy is an adaptation of the domestic marketing mix to meet foreign preferences and practices.

A classic example of a stage-three multidomestic company was Philips of the Netherlands in the 1960s. Philips, at that time, was a pure stage-three company. It relied upon relatively autonomous national organizations (NOs) in each country. Each NO developed its own strategy. This approach worked quite well for Philips until the company faced competition from Matsushita and other Japanese companies that had adopted global strategies. The difference in competitive advantage between Philips and its Japanese competitors was dramatic. Matsushita, for example, adopted a global strategy that focused its resources on serving a world market for home entertainment products.

In television receivers, Matsushita offered European customers two basic models based upon a single chassis. Philips, in contrast, offered European customers seven different models based on four different chassis. If the customers had demanded this variety, it would have made Philips a stronger competitor. Unfortunately for Philips, their product offering was not based upon customer demand. The customers wanted quality, features, and price. Philips' offering of greater variety in the technical design was based upon its structure and strategy. Each major country organization had its own engineering and manufacturing group, and, therefore, each major country came up with its own design and did its own manufacturing. This stage-three approach to product design and manufacturing was attractive to the Philips NOs, which enjoyed a high degree of autonomy. However, it was not attractive to Philips customers, who were looking for value as defined by features, performance, and price: They were getting more value from the company with a global strategy than from the multinational.

As the Matsushita strategy offered greater value to the customer, Philips saw itself losing market share. To meet the Japanese challenge, Philips decided to adopt a global strategy. The first step in this direction was to create what Philips called Industry Main Groups in the Netherlands. They were responsible for developing a global strategy for R&D, marketing, and manufacturing.

The decline of the multinational corporation is based upon this type of confrontation a thousand times over and the judge is the consumer: Because the global strategy has been creating more consumer value, it has been winning this contest.

Stage IV—The Global Corporation

A global corporation is much more than a company with investments and sales in many countries. There is no existing "pure" global company i.e., that meets all of the characteristics outlined below. Still, there are a growing number of companies that are evolving toward stage four.

Scanning or Information Acquisition. The stage-four company scans the world for opportunity and threat. Every company, regardless of the geographic scope of its current operations and regardless of its aspirations should be aware of what is happening in its industry and in markets globally. Knowledge about developments in markets, companies, capacity, and about economic, socio-cultural, political, and technological trends and developments is strategically important because it may suggest valuable ideas and approaches for a more creative strategy for the domestic market. It may also provide early warning of new competitive challenges in the domestic market.

Vision. This company is not content to think in terms of operating in a single national or even regional environment. It believes in the motto, "Grow or die!" Its aspiration are global: world markets, world customers, and world-scale competitors.

It is not necessary for every executive of the global company to have global vision. If the CEO does not have global vision, however, its presence in the lower ranks of the company will not really make much of a difference.

Without global vision, a company will not seek and find the opportunities that will enable it to become global. Before action comes aspiration. The hubris and aspiration of U.S. companies in the 1960s and of Japanese companies in the 1980s has been a major driving force behind U.S. and Japanese global expansion.

Geographic Scope. What a company does with the information generated by a strategic global scanning and environmental assessment depends upon its strategy alternatives. The best strategy is to concentrate its forces to ensure that real customer value and competitive superiority are achieved in each target market. Clearly, not every company should operate globally. Indeed, many should limit the geographic scope of their operations to a single country or even to a single region within a country.

Also, a company does not have to extend its operating configuration to many countries in order to have a global strategy. What every CEO must do is to ensure that strategic scanning is global. With such information, each company is in a position to formulate its own best competitive strategy, which will include the company's decision about the geographic scope of its operations.

Operating style. Recently a global panel of experts on company strategy selected IBM and Coca Cola as the top two companies with global marketing strategies. Both companies are mature and established global marketers who have demonstrated great skill in merging corporate vision and in-depth market knowledge. In both companies, key functions such as finance, research and development, new product development, product management, and purchasing are integrated on a global basis. In IBM, for example, all R&D is part of a global effort. There is no such thing as U.S. or French R&D in IBM. Technology is universal, and the customer base served with the applied technologies is global. Therefore, R&D is part of a single IBM program that is dispersed geographically but integrated functionally. This integrated style replaces the decentralized, bottom-up style of the multinational and the centralized top-down style of the international company.

Marketing. A basic marketing issue faced by every company is whether to extend the marketing mix "as is," that is, to take whatever is offered in the home country and offer that same product, price, advertisement, and so on to the foreign market, or to adapt the home country marketing mix to local differences, or to create a new marketing mix for a global market. The stage-two company extends its marketing mix. The stage-three company adapts its marketing mix. In contrast, the stage-four company extends, adapts, and creates a marketing mix. The global corporation extends products when appropriate. An example is RJR-Nabisco's Camel cigarette brand. This product was a local brand in many countries when the company decided to try to develop it as a world brand. The strongest Camel position was in Germany. On a country-by-country basis, RJR-Nabisco was able to extend the positioning of Camel in Germany to other European countries and then to the world.

The global corporation adapts products and the marketing mix where appropriate. Mercedes-Benz has positioned itself as a super luxury car in North America and in much of the world outside Europe. In Germany and its neighboring countries, Mercedes is a basic automobile. The export model of the Mercedes-Benz is the same car with an option package. This is an example of adapting the marketing strategy to take advantage of an opportunity for advantageous positioning.

Some products require no adaptation or change whatsoever. BIC's line of pens, butane lighters, and razors, for example, is identical worldwide. They serve their customers' basic need to draw lines, make flames, and cut hair. The only changes BIC makes in its products are in the packaging in order to take advantage of local supplier materials and market preferences concerning quantity. Nevertheless, BIC finds that success in a market depends critically on the marketing skill and talent of the local manager who must adapt BIC's pricing, promotion, and channel strategy to the competitive and market conditions in his/her country.

Creation is the development of a new product for an identified market. In the case of the global corporation, this market may be global, and the creation may be a global brand if it is a consumer product. An excellent example of a global brand is the Sony Walkman. The Walkman is personal portable sound.

The original idea for this product was suggested to Mr. Morita, the Chairman of Sony, by a golfing partner. Mr. Morita believed that the demand for personal portable sound was global and decided to introduce the Walkman as a global product instead of using the country-by-country approach of earlier eras.

In some industries, such as pharmaceuticals, the only justification for the enormous expenditures and long development and testing times for new products is a global market. A single country market, even if it is a large country like the United States, is not big enough to pay back the cost of developing a new product.

The global-strategy company measures its market and competitive performance on a national and a global basis. Many companies say they are global-strategy companies and then describe their competitive position in the home market or vis-a-vis home country industry competitors. This is an almost certain indication that the company's real strategy is international or multinational. General Motors for example is not a global corporation. Its focus is on its share of the U.S. market and its market position vis-a-vis Chrysler and Ford. The global measure would be market share and competitive position in the worldwide automotive industry, including, of course, the major Japanese and European competitors.

Human resource policy. The global corporation does not have a national bias in the selection and assignment of people. Its rule is simple: Pick the best person for the job. The same rule applies to the development of human resources. The best people, regardless of nationality, are developed for key positions everywhere in the world. This is in contrast to the international company which reserves top positions worldwide for home country nationals, and to the multinational company, which reserves top jobs in each host country for host country nationals.

Purchasing. The global company purchases its product from the best source worldwide. This does not necessarily mean going to the lowest-wage or even to the lowest-cost country. The best source may be a factory located in a high-wage advanced country that achieves world low-cost producer status on the basis of automation and efficiency, or it may be from a home or host country that is not the lowest-cost source but which values the company's contribution to the countries' welfare by creating jobs.

Preferred form of partnership. The history of joint ventures by stage-two and stage-three companies is one of relatively high instability. International and multinational companies enter into joint ventures with foreign partners to take advantage of combined resources and experience in addressing business opportunities. These are typically created to address a single country opportunity, often the home country of one of the partners.

Today, the global corporation is careful to screen potential alliances to ensure that they fit the company's global strategic plan. These alliances, or global strategic partnerships (GSPs), are distinguished from stage-two and stage-three joint ventures because they are part of a global strategic design and not a single country effort. The lesson from experience with partnerships is clear: Partners should do their best to form compatible and complementary marriages that bring the necessary resources and energy to a project. Partners should also be realistic and recognize that not all marriages succeed. A prenuptial agreement is an excellent idea because it paves the way for a relatively simple separation should the two parties find it difficult or impossible to work with each other. For example, Rupert Murdoch's News Corporation's successful partnership with Hachette to launch new ELLE and PREMIER magazines in the United States and in the U.K. provides that if the partners cannot agree on an issue of importance to the joint business, the partners will dissolve their relationship with a buyout, with the flip of a coin deciding who buys and who sells.

Global Success Story

Murdoch's News Corporation Ltd. is an excellent example of an emerging global corporation. It now spans three continents and is expanding from its strong base in newspaper and magazine and database print products to establish a position as a major television broadcaster in Australia, the United States, and Europe as a programming producer. Some observers believe Murdoch has demonstrated vision and an ability to see around corners. He recognizes that print's share of advertising revenue is declining, causing him to establish a major position in television broadcasting and in the production of broadcast products for television stations. His acquisitions have tapped world financial markets, and have been supported by the cross-subsidization of investments (cash from the U.K. has been poured into the United States to finance the acquisition of television stations and of 20th Century Fox) and by the transfer of experienced executives and editors across national boundaries.

Murdoch's ELLE is one of the most successful magazine launches in the U.S. fashion book market in 25 years. ELLE's success is based on the powerful combination that the global corporation assembles: Vision at the top; the common touch and "feel" for customers and markets; experienced U.S. magazine editors, publishers, and staff; financial resources and commitment to see the new launch through the early net negative cash flow years; and an editorial director from the French ELLE to assist in transferring the flavor and feel of the original ELLE to the new American ELLE.

If you don't know where you're going, goes the old adage, any road will take you there. Today, every company should know where it is on the typology of stages of corporate development, what it is becoming. This corporate self knowledge will pay big dividends by ensuring that the firm is doing the best possible job of creating value for customers. Global companies and global strategies are winning because they outperform their predecessors in this vital dimension. In the increasingly open and competitive markets of the world, it is the customers, not the vested interests, who are deciding who is winning and who is losing.

The Japanese Experience

Sukeyuki Inaba
President
Asahi Chemical Industry America, Inc.

An urgent telex arrived at our headquarters in Japan the other day. The K.G.B. had arrested three foreign businessmen in Moscow: a Frenchman, a Japanese, and an American. All were sentenced to death. But the judge said that in keeping with the spirit of Glasnost, each would be allowed one reasonable last wish. So, the Frenchman requested a fine meal with a chanteuse; the Japanese man said, "I want to give a speech on our glorious achievements in productivity"; and the American shouted, "Kill me before I have to hear another speech on productivity!"

My topic is not productivity. It is the Japanese industry's evolving strategic planning process. Strategic planning helps find the right things to do; it focuses on effectiveness. Productivity assumes that you know both what to do and how to do it; it focuses on efficiency.

In discussing the evolving trends of strategic planning in Japan, I will use Asahi Chemical as an example, since it is reasonably representative of large, diverse Japanese firms that operate internationally. To illustrate how strategic planning has evolved in Japan, I will give a brief overview of Asahi Chemical's experience over the last three decades.

Four distinct phases divide these years of development. For each, I'll describe the nature of the change, how our planning process altered, and what our key strategies and results were. Surviving and exploiting these profound breaks with the past forced major revisions in our planning and operations.

I. The 1960-1973 **High-Growth Phase**

After recovering from World War II, Japanese industry entered a period of seemingly unlimited growth opportunities. With the emergence of free trade, a worldwide economic upturn, and growing business optimism, Asahi entered a period of remarkable expansion. Most of our present products and processes were developed in these years.

During this period, our CEO's role was that of an exemplar, or "sensei." A sensei is not only a master of a chosen field but also an expert and enthusiastic teacher of that subject. Long-range planning in this phase was "bottom-up," with each team striving to achieve its target. Our plans were developed by front-

Phase I	
PERIOD:	1960-1973
PHASE CHANGE:	Seemingly unlimited global growth potential
CEO's ROLE:	Exemplar (Sensei)
PLANNING PROCESS:	Bottom-up
KEY STRATEGIES:	1. Horizontal integration 2. Diversification 3. Backward integration
MAJOR RESULTS:	Sales—$.3 billion (1960) to $2.9 billion (1973)
CONCLUSION:	"Make hay while the sun shines but be ready to take shelter."

line executives in production and sales. They proposed their plans to divisional managers, who reviewed, coordinated, revised, and made recommendations to top management.

Combining the strategies of integration and diversification, Asahi grew from a local cellulose fiber producer to one of Japan's biggest fiber and chemical companies. Asahi employed:

- horizontal integration into fibers such as acrylic, nylon, and polyester;
- diversification (in some cases through Asahi-Dow) into chemical resins, plastics, films, construction, housing, pharmaceuticals, and foods;
- backward integration toward raw materials; and
- forward integration toward the customer.

Sales rose nearly ten-fold in these years.

II. The 1974-1980 **Periods of Adjustment**

During this time, Japan was plagued by slow growth and uncertainty. The two oil crises caused severe damage to Japan's heavy industry, especially because Japanese firms must import so much.

To survive this difficult period, Asahi had to first restore profit levels by streamlining and then improve its financial structure by lowering fixed costs.

Phase II

PERIOD:	1974-1980
PHASE CHANGE:	Traumatic raw material shortages
CEO's ROLE:	Autocrat
PLANNING PROCESS:	Top-Down
KEY STRATEGIES:	1. Rationalization 2. Cost minimization 3. Planting & watering the seeds for future profits
MAJOR RESULTS:	1. Employment cutbacks of 5,000 or 25% 2. Total Savings = $400 million
CONCLUSION:	"Leave no stone unturned BUT always remember to plant and water the seeds for future profits." Prior integration & diversification paid off

These requirements forced us into a strong "top-down" planning process, whether we liked it or not. Decisions from a central authority that was aware of the overall picture were essential to begin fast corrective action. During the years 1975 to 1981, Asahi was successful in curtailing labor, energy, and transportation expenditures. The total savings amounted to $400 million (in 1981 dollars).

The strategy of diversification followed in the previous phase supported Asahi in these years. The first oil crisis seriously hurt the fiber and textile businesses, but our petrochemical plant came on-stream in time to provide good earnings. During the second oil crisis, the loss of petrochemical products was offset by profits from engineering plastics, fine chemical, and housing and construction materials.

III. 1981-1986 **Efficiency and New Technology**

In these years Japanese industry looked toward the next two decades and so emphasized new technoloy and new product development. But our industry also became aware of resource limitations—of people and of funds. As a result, companies like ours strove to turn around "loss" businesses and to establish priorities for R&D projects.

Phase III

PERIOD:	1981-1986
PHASE CHANGE:	Return to Growth
CEO's ROLE:	Innovator
PLANNING PROCESS:	Integration of bottom up with top down
KEY STRATEGIES:	1. Interdivisional New Asahi Creation (NAC) Programs (3 yr. turnarounds as needed & R&D priorities) 2. Project 2001
MAJOR RESULTS:	1. Internal turnaround experts developed & they ended the $100 Million loss in 3 years 2. New R&D thrusts in biotechnology & electronics 3. Accelerated R&D for energy & new, high-performance materials
CONCLUSION:	"Inspire future leaders' commitment by encouraging their major involvement in strategic planning." Both expertise & information are vital to solve problems or exploit opportunities effectively & quickly.

Planning at Asahi at this time combined bottom-up and top-down styles. As part of a top-down approach, our president, K. Miyazaki, rotated several executive vice presidents into positions as temporary heads of different divisions. Each made a thorough review of a division and gained broader experience. Losses were eliminated within three years in this interdivisional effort, called the New Asahi Creation Program.

The bottom-up planning process was exemplified by "Projects 2001," launched in 1984 and designed to identify business prospects for the 21st century. A survey was sent to 400 young managers and assistant managers (those who would not reach retirement age before the year 2001), asking for new product ideas. Two project teams followed up on these suggestions. Each team consisted of an executive vice president, a director, and 20 of the 400 young managers. Each sent strategic plans to top management covering areas such as R&D and allocation of resources.

These proposals led to strategic decisions, including: (1) Biotechnology projects should receive more management resources; (2) An electronics laboratory should be established for basic research in new areas; and (3) R&D efforts devoted to energy and raw materials should be accelerated.

IV. 1987-? **Dynamic Uncertainties**

The dollar-yen relationship has a dramatic impact on industrial development, and the future is difficult to forecast. Uncertainties that affect Japanese industry include the "twin deficts" in the United States, the budget and trade deficits, which may influence the course of the world economy.

To maintain flexibility in the face of uncertainty, Asahi's planning process and strategies changed once again. We began to think that we had overemphasized the creation of new businesses out of R&D efforts at the expense of realizing the full potential of existing businesses. We must blend the two: breed the next generation of businesses and support existing businesses. Asahi is pursuing this more balanced combination of strategies through an empahsis on three-year planning at the divisional level.

These strategies, approved by top management, involve reinforcing existing businesses by:

Phase IV

PERIOD:	1987-??
PHASE CHANGE:	Era of Dynamic Environmental Uncertainties
CEO's ROLE:	Patriarch
PLANNING PROCESS:	Emphasis on divisions & a 3-year horizon
KEY STRATEGIES:	1. Strengthen today's businesses for faster & less costly growth & development in the future 2. Invest in new businesses & technologies 3. Harvest from past R&D while planting & watering new seed for future profits
MAJOR RESULTS:	???
CONCLUSION:	Comprehensive planning is the only way we have to handle major changes

- Expanding the market for and uses of existing products;
- Promoting mid- and downstream activity; and
- Developing innovations in process, automation, and cost-saving techniques.

Our three-year strategies also emphasize earlier launches of new projects (including joint ventures, equity positions, and takeovers); more efficient use of R&D; and investment levels just above the amount of self-financing ($1.9 billion over three years).

Conclusions

At Asahi we can point to at least one major lesson from each phase. From the first, a period of enormous growth, we learned to "make hay while the sun shines"—but to be ready to take shelter. In the second phase marked by shortages and slow growth, it was important to "leave no stone unturned"—but to remember to plant and water the seed for future growth. As we returned to growth in the third phase, it was clear that both information and expertise were vital for solving problems and for exploiting opportunities quickly and effectively. And we learned that it is important to inspire future leaders. Finally, in the present uncertain phase, we have realized that comprehensive planning is the only way we know to handle major changes. Furthermore, no single planning process or strategy survives a change from one phase to another. More broadly, in Japanese industry strategic planning is typically: (1) an entrenched part of all executives' responsibilities (it has been for decades); (2) a slow but thorough process that can nonetheless be quickly implemented; (3) heavily influenced by MITI (Japan's Ministry of International Trade & Investment), tradition, and (4) multinational operation; and driven by a need to "win with ease," since waste and big mistakes are unaffordable luxuries.